Dr. Jim Grassi has always had a heart for men and he proves it everyday. He has written so much to challenge men to take their God-given place so that the family, the church, and the culture can become more like what God intended. I am praying that men will read this book and heed the call so that those in our slice of history will see something different in us and want what we have.

Jim Putman, Senior Pastor
Real Life Ministries, Post Falls, Idaho

As a pastor, I often feel torn between the polarization in our society. There are those who would like to see the church accommodating to all lifestyles and those who would like the church to be an extension of a particular political party. How do we discern the place of balance where we stand strongly on biblical virtues and simultaneously welcome those who don't know Jesus (and don't live or think like those who do know Jesus) with open arms? Jim Grassi helps us on the journey of finding our place standing in the gap!

Dr. Kent Mankins,
Valley Assembly, Spokane Valley, WA

Dr. Jim Grassi has been at this ministry to men since 1981. His exhortations and encouragement to men are the same medicine he has taken and walked out his adult life. I've known Jim over four decades, and I can truthfully say he has been faithful at his post, and faithful to the call God has extended to him. My hope is that the readers of this book will see the beauty and depth of wisdom Jim extends to us here in these pages. Gentlemen, we don't have a day when we can any longer be passive. Let us shake off the dust of complacency, the doubts about whether God is on the move - stand up and step into those gaps and see the Kingdom manifested in our midst! To the King and the Kingdom, and "sighters who see."

Jeff Klippenes, LMFT, Castro Valley, CA

The Watchman is a must-read book for all men regardless of age, ethnicity, or religious background. Dr Grassi pulls no punches while addressing many of the issues that contribute to the radical and depraved change in our moral compass. He spells out the epidemic Satanic plagues impacting much of our society. There's no doubt that if men would step up, read *The Watchman*, pay attention to Dr. Grassi's words, and apply them, it would have a positive outcome in the direction our young men are taking today.

Pastor Dave Mortara, Retired, Queen Creek, AZ

The Watchman

THE
WATCHMAN

A Clarion Call for Men to Stand in the Gap

Jim Grassi, D.MIN.

The Watchman

©2023 Dr. Jim Grassi

ISBN 978-1-7358693-3-9

DEDICATION

I dedicate this book to faithful and courageous watchmen like my friend and editor, Rob Fischer. Rob is willing to say tough things during times when others turn their backs and decline to get involved. He is a faithful husband, father, and follower of Jesus Christ. Rob is a kind-hearted man with great wisdom who can project his opinions in a loving manner. To God be all the glory!

I also commit this project to couples like Bill and Judi Williams who stand in the gap for family, friends, and their church. Their generous hearts and amazing commitment to fighting for the fundamental Judeo/Christian values of our culture is awe inspiring. I especially appreciate Judi's careful editing of this manuscript. May they and their family be blessed and follow the examples Bill and Judi have set for all of us to follow.

To God be the glory!

TABLE OF CONTENTS

The Wall Has Been Breached

The Need for Real Leaders

Standing in the Gap for Biblical Manhood

Standing in the Gap for Your Family

Standing in the Gap in the Marketplace

FOREWORD

The Great Battleground

The great battleground of our modern generation is for Truth and the warriors chosen to defend that truth at all cost. These warriors are men of God. Over the last few generations, our dear and faithful female counterparts have had to take a greater role of standing for the truth to raise children in the truth. However, God's Word is clear from start to finish that proper, loving, spiritual authority has been delegated to men. It is time for men to take up that mantle and stand for truth as leaders in the home, the church and our communities.

We men find it quite natural to lock our doors and windows and defend our homes from intruders at night, but too often in our distraction or exhaustion, we fail to guard the spiritual doors and windows of our homes. Too often these days, homes full of God's children have no male protector at all. To often, board rooms and school boards are filled with the voices of contrary agendas and there is no man to stand in the gap for biblical values.

We as men are the ones God has called to stand in the gap when truth is being torn down. We are the ones to faithfully face backlash from the world. We are not to "stand in the path of sinners," but we are to stand in harm's way to face the battle head on. It is not hyperbole to say that the fate of future generations depends on men currently alive to stand our ground for truth, God's Truth.

Dear reader, Dr. Jim Grassi has not written this book to shame men but to encourage men that we have a role to play and a calling to answer. Will you sound the alarm as the watchmen of old? Will you and I and the men of this generation stand up for truth and stand in breaches of the family's wall? One such watchman sounding the alarm is Dr. Grassi, and I believe this pivotal book, *The Watchman – A Clarion Call for Men to Stand in the Gap*, is not only timely, but critical to awaken the role of men to lead God's way. Let us stand in the gap and be counted as faithful men, godly men, family men as husbands and fathers. May this book be a blessing to you and generations to come.

In Christ Jesus our Lord,
Dave Love,
Pastor of Calvary Castle Rock, and
Regional Leader, Calvary Chapel Association

INTRODUCTION

Has our society gone mad? Have we totally lost our way from the vision our forefathers had in developing this country? We are beginning to look like the evil nations of the Old Testament or a Soviet-bloc nation from the 60s.

In the 1950s, *Popeye the Sailor Man* was a popular cartoon series. As a boy, I remember coming home from school and fantasizing about being the kind of hero and ambassador for good that Popeye represented in his battles with evil.

One of Popeye's favorite expressions in his quirky sailor talk was, "That's all I can stands, 'cause I can't stands no more!" Popeye lived by a strong moral code that he guarded fearlessly. He was a watchman protecting the helpless and innocent.

In our past, there have been other such heroes, both fictional and real: Superman, Roy Rogers, Gene Autry, John Wayne, Winston Churchill, Theodore "Teddy" Roosevelt, Ronald Reagan, and Martin Luther King, Jr. These heroes were all men of principle. They were men who stood for what is right and served others selflessly. They too were watchmen.

I wrote my book, *Act Like Men – Be Strong,* during a time when the progressive movement was taking form and was challenging authentic, biblical manhood. The antagonists labeled strong, moral men who were leaders in their homes, churches, and the workplace "toxic masculinity," and blamed them for most of the social ills in the country, even including global warming!

In that book, I proposed that there are two primary factors that feed the antagonism toward men. The first is *the failure of men to pursue godliness.* Overall, we men have fallen asleep at the wheel. We've gone the way of the world. We are not salt and light in this world as Christ charged us to be.

The second factor is *an angry group of people who are socially and politically liberal.* This group is intent on destroying the very fabric of our country by calling good evil and evil good.

I believed that society couldn't get any farther away from God than what I was seeing in 2019. But I was wrong! The continued slide towards insanity and corrupt thinking has swelled to an avalanche of immorality threatening to overwhelm even our young, innocent children.

We now have teachers who feel compelled to tell a five or six-year-old child they don't have to feel or act like their biological identity. School boards are imposing suspension from school if a child uses the wrong pronoun for a classmate who identifies as a different gender. A school nurse can now guide teenagers to have a sex change operation without the consent of their parents. Doctors who are unwilling to perform the "chemical castration" of children are now breaking the law President Biden signed into force.

Disney used to be the bastion of decency and strong morals when it came to children's entertainment. Now Disney has eliminated the use of personal pronouns and sex determination for its characters. Disney is bent on convincing our children that such gender dysphoria is normal. The transgender mayor of Palm Springs has promised to allocate $200,000 to develop a guaranteed income pilot program for transgender and nonbinary residents. And the insanity goes on.

The term "woke" is the new designation for those who are hyper-vigilant and hyper-extreme in their efforts to promote radical Marxism and so-called progressive views on practically everything. Though they say things like, "Follow the science," they balk at real science and operate in a fantasy world of their own making. Logic and truth have been trampled on.

This Woke agenda has been thrust upon our educational institutions, political process, businesses, and even upon some churches. The left pushes their woke agenda under the guise of social justice and love, while slandering, censoring, and silencing anyone who opposes them—so much for love and justice.

Wokeism is a cancel culture and a form of Marxism that breeds chaos. We can no longer have a civil and respectful discourse on issues like abortion, drugs, social justice, gun control, or any other political idea without being labeled a racist, bigot, or MAGA advocate.

The Woke Movement believes that anyone who disagrees with them should be ostracized, vilified, and censored. Now there is institutional suppression and pressure on icons like movie stars, athletes, and business leaders because some Woke person might feel oppressed by their positions. Anyone who *feels* oppressed is now by definition oppressed.

This crazy movement wants to determine what makes up free speech. People believe they are their own authority, so we don't need police, law and order, or other governmental controls in our life. It is sad today that according to a recent report over 60% of the people in this country are now afraid to openly express their opinions or feelings on important matters, such as faith, because they don't want to be publicly labeled or called out by someone who disagrees with their opinions.

Most importantly these same people discount God and the Bible. They do not want to be accountable to God or anyone else.

The Apostle Peter wrote of them:

> [They] … despise authority. Reckless, self-centered, they speak abusively of angelic majesties without trembling, … using abusive speech where they have no knowledge, … They count it a pleasure to revel in

the daytime. They are stains and blemishes, reveling in their deceptions as they feast with you, having eyes full of adultery that never cease from sin, … accursed children; … These are springs without water and mists driven by a storm, for whom the black darkness has been reserved. These are springs without water and mists driven by a storm, for whom the black darkness has been reserved. For, while speaking out arrogant words of no value they entice by fleshly desires, by indecent behavior, those who barely escape from the ones who live in error, promising them freedom while they themselves are slaves of corruption. (2 Peter 2:10-19 *select portions*)

In the book of Genesis we see a similar type of behavior among people during the days of Noah. People stopped acknowledging and obeying God's plan for mankind.

Then the Lord saw that the wickedness of mankind was great on the earth, and that every intent of the thoughts of their hearts was only evil continually. So the Lord was sorry that He had made mankind on the earth, and He was grieved in His heart. Then the Lord said, "I will wipe out mankind whom I have created from the face of the land; mankind, and animals as well, and crawling things, and the birds of the sky. For I am sorry that I have made them." But Noah found favor in the eyes of the Lord. (Genesis 6:5-8)

To some extent, I think we men must assume some of the responsibility for what has happened in our country. Too many of us have become lazy and uninvolved with the leadership in our homes, churches, and communities. For many of us, our passions, careers, and hobbies have distracted us from our first love and responsibility to Christ and our family.

In the book of Jeremiah, we see the evidence of too many men stepping away from their God-given roles as leaders of the home and letting the women and government take control of their lives and families. God stated then what I believe to be true today, "Their course is evil And their might is not right" (Jeremiah 23:10b).

Like many of you reading this, I fear for our nation, our churches, and our families. But while things have gotten worse than any other time in my lifetime, when I read the Scriptures, I recognize that there have been other awful times like this as well.

In the sixth century B.C., the nation of Judah (the southern two tribes of Israel) had become so wicked for so long that God finally had enough. They had abandoned justice and truth. They had forsaken the One True God and chased after a myriad of false gods. They sacrificed their children to these gods. They cheated and took advantage of the poor, and they practiced all kinds of sexual sins and perversions.

And to top it off, they had groomed their own "woke" prophets to promote their evil ways and silence anyone who disagreed with them. Does this sound familiar?

As I said, God finally had enough, so He used another godless nation, the Babylonians, to punish Judah. The Babylonians led by Nebuchadnezzar mounted a long, bloody war against Judah and captured Jerusalem. They carried off the fittest of the survivors to Babylon to serve Nebuchadnezzar there. One of those well-known captives was Ezekiel, who was both a prophet and a priest.

While he was among the exiles in Babylonia, God appointed Ezekiel to be a prophet and a watchman. The Lord said to him:

> Then He said to me, "Son of man, I am sending you to the sons of Israel, to a rebellious people who have rebelled against Me; they and their fathers have revolted against Me to this very day. So I am sending you to those who are impudent and obstinate children, and you shall say to them, 'This is what the Lord God says:' As for them, whether they listen or not—for they are a rebellious house—they will know that a prophet has been among them. And as for you, son of man, you are not to fear them nor fear their words, though thistles and thorns are

with you and you sit on scorpions; you are not to fear their words nor be dismayed at their presence, since they are a rebellious house." (Ezekiel 2:3-6)

Then, in Ezekiel 3:17, the Lord said to Ezekiel, "Son of man, I have appointed you as a watchman for the house of Israel; whenever you hear a word from My mouth, warn them from Me." Ezekiel was to warn the people of Israel about their sin and its consequences. The Lord's desire was for them to repent, turn to Him, and put their faith in Him.

The Hebrew word for *watchman* comes from the word *shamar*, which means "to keep guard, observe, give heed, to watch for, to wait for." As stated in Isaiah 62:6, "I have posted watchmen on your walls, Jerusalem; they will never be silent day or night. You who call on the LORD, give yourselves no rest, and give him no rest till he establishes Jerusalem and makes her the praise of the earth". This suggest that we are to be vigilant in every way even when it could cost us some inconvenience or lack of rest.

In a similar way, the Lord has called us men as *watchmen*. He has tasked us with making disciples of all nations. As men who know and follow Jesus, we have a responsibility and calling to represent Christ well to those around us. We are to warn them of the consequences of their sins and God's judgment to come. We are to share the good news of forgiveness of sins through Jesus Christ and urge them to forsake their sins and follow the Lord.

But this holy calling to be a watchman and to make disciples must begin in our homes. Perhaps this is where we as men have failed the most. For unless we are guarding our families from evil and leading them closer to the Lord through our words and examples, then we have no business telling strangers how Jesus Christ can change their lives.

The Lord lamented in Ezekiel 22:30, " I searched for a man among them who would build up a wall and stand in the gap before Me for the land, so that I would not destroy it; but I found no one." (NKJV) The men of Ezekiel's day had become apathetic.

In his book, *Is This the End?* Dr. David Jeremiah demonstrates that as a nation, we too have become apathetic. And "when a nation drifts into apathy, it also drifts into unrestrained indulgence of appetites."[1] And this is precisely where we find ourselves today.

This book is meant to be a clarion call to men everywhere to assume the role as a *watchman*. For decades, men in general have shirked their responsibilities in the home as husbands and fathers. Remove the watchmen and the city is easily overtaken and conquered. We have left our posts. We have abandoned our wives and our children.

It is time for godly men to take a stand for Christ and the values He taught and become *watchmen* for their families,

---

1   Dr. David Jeremiah, *Is This the End?* (W. Publishing Group, Nashville, TN, 2016), p. 108.

churches, and communities. If you and I don't become pro-active in alerting people to the dangers of our progressive culture, who will? Who will lead the charge against the tyranny and depravity that is overtaking our nation? Our hope and the answer to our situation is not a political one, but a spiritual one and a very practical one – one in which we can each make a difference.

You might say, "The country is too far gone, what's the use?" Or "There's not much we can do but wait until Jesus comes." Or "What can I do to make a difference when evil is so widespread and pervasive?"

Historian Edward Everett Hale had the following response to those questions, "I am only one, but still, I am one. I cannot do everything, but I can do something. And because I cannot do everything, I will not refuse to do something that I can do."

Who will lead the charge against the tyranny and deprav-ity that is overtaking our nation? As the Lord seeks today for a man who will stand in the gap before Him, will He find such a man? Will you resolve to be such a man? I hope so! Continue reading to see how you can join a movement of men who will "stand in the gap" and serve as watchmen for Christ.

"Only in heaven will we be perfect and without sin, because only in heaven will we become like Christ."

– Billy Graham

CHAPTER 1

The Wall Has Been Breached

"Then the Lord saw that the wickedness of mankind was great on the earth, and that every intent of the thoughts of their hearts was only evil continually."

– Genesis 6:5 –

On the night Jesus was betrayed, after eating the Passover meal with His disciples and spending considerable time teaching them, they left the Upper Room and made their way in the dark to the Mount of Olives where they had been staying. It was late and the disciples were tired, but Jesus knew what would transpire that night, so He singled out Peter, James, and John and asked them to watch with Him while He went a bit farther, dropped to His knees and prayed.

Knowing that He would be condemned to death and be crucified, bearing the sins of all mankind, His soul was in great distress. Three times He came back to the three disciples He had put on watch, and three times He found them sleeping. He kept urging them, "Watch and pray, lest you enter into temptation." But each time they fell asleep.

The fourth time Jesus came back to them and found them sleeping again, He roused them and said, "Are you still sleeping and resting? Behold, the hour is at hand, and the Son of Man is being betrayed into the hands of sinners. Rise, let us be going. See, My betrayer is at hand" (Matthew 26:45-46 NKJV).

Men, we must not be too hard on the disciples. They were mere men. It was late. It was dark and the text says, "Their eyes were heavy." And I believe that, like Peter, James, and John, many of us have been lulled into a less-than-watchful state.

There is a great leadership void in our country and in the world right now as there was in Ezekiel's day. Such a void is ripe for the rise of the Antichrist, but we do not know when he will appear. This leadership void begs to be filled and right now men and women without any moral compass are scrambling to fill that void with their so-called progressive agendas.

Their progressive agendas denounce God, the Bible, and everything we hold to be good, righteous, and just. They may speak of love, justice, and fairness, but it's always at the expense of someone else. They tout *tolerance* as their primary value, except that they are adamantly intolerant of anyone who doesn't hold to their position. Tolerance only works in one direction for them. They demand, "You be tolerant of me, or else!"

They claim to be purveyors of truth, but their truth is whatever they fancy it to be. As far as they are concerned, two opposing claims can both be true, which defies the very definition of truth. They've reduced truth to any personal belief a person wants to conjure up.

Those who are trying to fill this leadership void are rewriting our history as well. They seek to portray all our forefathers as slave-owning bigots and racists. They want to rewrite our Constitution, stripping us of the God-given rights its writers sought to preserve.

Why is all this happening? Because there is a great leadership void. The Lord said, "So I sought for a man among them who would stand in the gap before Me, but I found no one."

Why are we allowing all this to happen? *Because we are not stepping up to fill that leadership void.* We have become too comfortable. We're too complacent. We've become apathetic. We enjoy our toys and time off and travel and TV shows. We don't want to lose any of that. We don't want to rock the boat. After all, there is a great price to pay if these woke leaders decide we pose too great a threat.

Gentlemen, like the disciples of Jesus on the night He was betrayed, we too are oblivious to what is about to happen. Our eyes have grown heavy. We're tired. And when the soldiers show up with spears and torches, we flee into the darkness hoping to go unnoticed in the confusion.

For decades, we men have been AWOL. So many of us have been unfaithful to our wives, if not in the act of adultery, then in divorce, or pornography, or simply not loving them sacrificially as Christ loves the church (Ephesians 5:25).

We've also been AWOL as far as our kids are concerned. Far too many children are growing up without a father at home. How can an absent dad "bring them up in the discipline and instruction of the Lord" (Ephesians 6:4)? Kids need to be with their fathers (*and* mothers). Children learn best by example. Dads, that should scare us, because our kids are watching us. They are great mimics. Remember the adage, "Like father, like son"?

Do you want your son or daughter to grow up like you? What values, what disciplines, what habits do you exemplify for them? Will they grow up to be more Christlike having watched your life and having listened to your speech?

Fathers, what do your children watch? What do they listen to? Who are their heroes? Who are their friends?

What kind of company do they keep? What are they doing when you're not watching?

Often, I've heard parents say, "I'm not going to make my kids go to church, because I want them to make their own life choices." That is foolish! You *are* making a choice for them, and a bad one it is! I'll have more to say about fatherhood in a later chapter.

Men, who are you at work? Do your co-workers know that you are a Christ follower? Do they see a difference in your life? Are you working at your job "as unto the Lord"? Are you doing anything at work that would embarrass you if your wife, your child, your pastor, or your boss found out?

I know this must be difficult to read, but please understand that I'm writing as much to myself as to anyone else who is reading this book.

Men, there is a great leadership void, and it has occurred because we've left our post. We have fallen asleep. We have been AWOL, so someone else has moved in to take over, to fill in the gap. And their agenda is not pretty.

We have become distracted by many things—some of them "shiny" and some of them simply the worries of this life. What does your relationship with Jesus Christ look like right now? In what areas are you struggling? Where are you winning? To what extent would Jesus come to you and declare, "Well done, good and faithful servant.

You have been faithful over a few things; I will put you in charge of many things"?

What has the Lord been showing you from His Word lately? What role does prayer play in your life and where do you see God answering your prayers? What other spiritual disciplines do you practice in order to grow in your relationship with Christ and declare Him before others? In what ways is your faith in the Lord greater today than it was a year ago, or ten years ago?

I'm not talking about keeping a set of strict rules and practices here. Nor am I trying to guilt anyone. Neither guilt nor shame are good motivators. Instead, what I'm talking about has to do with patterns of behavior that make for a healthy relationship between a man and his Lord, his family, and all others with whom he deals.

There is a great leadership void. There's a huge hole in the wall of our fortress and the Lord is looking for men to stand in the gap. Will you rise to the task?

Discussion Questions:

In what ways are you leading your wife and children closer to the Lord?

What other men in your life are benefiting from your fellowship and partnership with them?

Who are you discipling? Do you know how to disciple someone? (If not, read on because we'll show you how.)

"An engaged and loving father is the most powerful man-making force on the planet. The opposite is also true. When fathers are absent physically or emotionally, the wound that results is profound."

– Earl Hipp, Author

CHAPTER 2

The Need for Real Leaders

"Behold, the days are coming," declares the Lord, "When I will raise up for David a righteous branch; And He will reign as king and act wisely And do justice and righteousness in the land."

– Jeremiah 23:5 –

With all the senseless violence and mass murders in our country it causes me to reflect upon the 19 innocent elementary-age children and two school employees were gunned down by 18-year-old Salvador Ramos at Robb Elementary School in Uvalde, Texas on May

9

24, 2022. We're stunned at the senselessness, insanity, and raw evil of such a brutal act. Our hearts ache for the parents, siblings, and grandparents of these little children who were so mercilessly gunned down.

How could something like this happen? Where does such unbridled anger come from? How did we get here as a nation? What drives a young man to commit such evil?

Matt Walsh offered the following opinion: "Nearly all mass shootings, along with nearly all violence in our cities, trace directly back to kids raised in unstable families with absentee parents. So predictable that I knew it was the case with the Texas shooter before it was confirmed. Maybe we should talk about this."[2]

Is there something to Matt Walsh's observation, or was he just grabbing at straws for a possible answer in the face of such a horrible crime?

In *The Legacy of Absence: Resolving the Wounds from Uninvolved Fathers in Individuals, Families, and Society*, author Tim Olson begins his book with a similar bold statement, "There is clear evidence that all the problems in

2   Matt Walsh, "Traditional Family Matters," Instagram, May 24, 2022.

10

society can be traced back to fathers being uninvolved in the lives of their children."[3]

The 2019 United States Census figures indicate that nearly 19.7 million children were living in a home without a father. That translates to 26 percent of America's children living fatherless. Today, many reports suggest that the number is really around 50%. This renders America the most fatherless nation in the world.[4]

Olson explains further, "We know that father absence is the most critical social issue of our time because the majority of social problems correlate more strongly with fatherlessness than with *any other factor*, surpassing race, social class, and poverty."[5]

In case you're still not convinced about the crucial role fathers play in the lives of their children, consider the following data compiled by the National Center for Fathering.[6]

- Children who live in a home without a father are nearly four times more likely to be poor.

---

3   Tim Olson, *The Legacy of Absence: Resolving the Wounds from Uninvolved Fathers in Individuals, Families, and Society* (Minneapolis, MN: Tim Olson Life Coach, LLC, 2019), p. 1.

4   Olson, p. 26.

5   Olson, p. 44.

6   https://fathers.com/statistics-and-research/the-consequences-of-fatherlessness/

- Children with an absent father are dramatically more prone to drug and alcohol abuse.

- 71% of high school dropouts are fatherless.

- 63% of youth suicides occur in homes without a father.

- 80% of rapists grew up in a fatherless home.

- 85% of youth in prison had no father present in the home.

Keep in mind that these statistics don't even touch the issue of *how well* a father performs his paternal duties, but only whether he is present and involved.

Conflicting Priorities

On the one hand, we can recognize and agree with the problem of fatherlessness and the ills it fosters in our children and society. On the other hand, men feel caught in the vice-grip of the present-day culture that has lost its moral compass. Many politicians, the liberal media, Hollywood, and woke businesses promote deception, lies, and confusion about many things including the role of men. These entities would have us believe that strong, determined, compassionate, and courageous men are no longer welcome in our "progressive" culture.

Our culture is doing everything it can to sissify, belittle, and silence men. Added to that are the normal, everyday issues men face: challenges at work, job security, providing for their families, life transitions, mid-life crises, financial setbacks, inflation, and rising gas and food prices. And there are a host of other issues we men face.

But too many men respond poorly to these threats and other factors. Instead of being faithful to their wives and loving and caring for their children, they "look out for number one" – meaning themselves. And they abandon their family – if not physically, then emotionally.

Many men do have a keen sense of their responsibility to provide for their family. But they interpret "provide for" solely as a financial pursuit, oblivious to the need to provide a safe, loving, spiritual refuge for his wife and children. And this narrow interpretation of "provide for" soon becomes license to pursue one's career—even at the expense of one's family.

The factors that ruined the culture of Ezekiel's day are not altogether different from those we're experiencing today. Within that context the Lord declared, "I sought for a man among them who would make a wall and stand in the gap before Me on behalf of the land, that I should not destroy it; but I found no one" (Ezekiel 22:30 NKJV).

In Ezekiel's day, the walls of Jerusalem had been breached and torn down. There were large gaps in the wall that needed repairing and the people were vulnerable to attack. Men needed to repair the wall and while they were doing so, stand in the gaps to prevent the enemy from getting through.

In our case, the walls are figurative and represent godly morals and ethics – the safeguards for our families and society. These "walls" have been breached. There are huge gaps in the moral fabric of our society. Evil is now not only tolerated, but is promoted, taught, flaunted, and celebrated, and those who reject evil are persecuted.

Who are these watchmen that the Lord seeks? Who are these men who will stand in the gap for their families? They are men who exhibit authentic manhood.

What Is Authentic Manhood?

The dictionary defines *authentic* as that which is real, genuine, not fake. (In this book, we are using the terms authentic manhood, biblical manhood, and true manhood interchangeably.)

In some circles, men associate manhood with a ripped physique, the ability to dunk a basketball, or catch a touchdown pass. Others associate manhood with catching a record fish or shooting a big game animal with a bow and arrow. Others measure manhood and success by the size of their bank account or the number of boats and cars in their garage. Men seek to express their manhood in countless other ways as well. They evaluate their manhood based on success, power, fortune, or fame.

On the darker side of things, some men seek to show their manhood by their sexual conquests, by drinking alcohol to excess, by experimenting with drugs, by a leadership style that manipulates and controls others, or by bullying others and belittling those who don't participate in these activities.

But all the above are false measures of authentic manhood. Some of those measures are not necessarily evil but distort the essence of what it means to be an authentic man. Such accomplishments and pursuits may provide a false and temporary sense of personal gratification, but they all focus on *self-importance,* and they distract from what manhood really means.

What does authentic manhood mean?

A friend of mine inherited a very old violin from his grandmother. There was a label on the inside of the violin that claimed, "Stradivarius 1713." Stradivarius violins were made by the Italian craftsman Antonio Stradivari in the late 1600s and early 1700s. One such violin sold for $16 million, and others for well over $1 million.

Experts believe there are about 600 Stradivarius violins still in existence, but only 244 have been accounted for. So, you can imagine the excitement my friend felt when he became the proud owner of his grandmother's violin!

There was only one problem... his violin was a fake, a cheap replica made by an inferior craftsman at a much later date. After having it appraised at three different antique houses, the experts all agreed it was only worth maybe $100 dollars but would require some repair.

In the same way, society has distorted what authentic manhood looks like. Our culture has presented us with a fake, a cheap replica of true manhood. Consequently, many men feel lost and confused. And the conditioning starts with the very young. Today, schools teach to the lowest common denominator insisting that everyone deserves a "participation trophy." This has robbed younger men of their desire to excel. "What's the use if there's no benefit in trying my best?" This approach also graduates students who are uneducated and ill-prepared for life in general. They become the "dumb guy" we see in sitcoms.

We also know that fatherlessness is an ever-growing problem. We've all heard the adage, "Like father, like son," and it holds true with fatherlessness as well. Charles Kettering wrote, "Every father should remember one day his son will follow his example, not his advice."

So, we find ourselves in a vicious cycle. How did we get where we are? How did authentic manhood become so distorted? It's because we men allowed the enemy to breech the walls. And when the walls were breeched, we did not stand in the gap to defend our families or the morals and principles that would protect them.

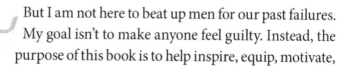

But I am not here to beat up men for our past failures. My goal isn't to make anyone feel guilty. Instead, the purpose of this book is to help inspire, equip, motivate, and educate men on what authentic, biblical manhood looks like and how-to live-in light of that as watchmen who stand in the gap for their families, churches, and communities.

God's Ideal for Men

Genesis 1:27 states, "So God created man in His own image, in the image of God He created him; male and female He created them." The essence of "True Manhood" is the reflection of a loving God who created man and woman in His image. With God there is no confusion about gender, sex, or family roles.

Genesis 2:24 clarifies further, "For this reason a man shall leave his father and his mother, and be joined to his wife; and they shall become one flesh." God gave us the model and plan for mankind and for marriage. But due to the lies and deception of the evil one, mankind rebelled against God. We doubted the goodness and plan of God and believed the lie of Satan. And we've operated under the lies of the evil one ever since.

Jesus said this about the evil one, "… he is a liar and the father of lies" (John 8:44). And "The thief comes only to steal and kill and destroy" (John 10:10). In the Garden of Eden, Satan tempted Eve. But there is every evidence from the text that Adam was present but passive as this occurred. He should have stepped into that gap. He should have intervened and protected his wife. But he didn't, and here we are today perpetuating this generational pattern.

17

For the most part, contemporary society and its broken-
ness can be directly linked to the failure of men to stand
firm in the gap as watchmen. This has resulted in fatherless
families or families where dad is not emotionally involved
in leading his tribe. Consequently, there is a direct link to a
myriad of social ills such as: homelessness, juvenile delin-
quency, pornography, poverty, crime, orphans, homosexuality, alcoholism, drug abuse, and a host of other emotional
disorders and addictions.

These problems are generational in nature. Consequently,
men today struggle with their roles as a leader, shepherd, protector, encourager, and provider for their families, because
their fathers failed to provide them with a good example.

I've worked in ministry to men for over four decades. I've
seen the confusion and disorientation men are experiencing today, and I've personally struggled with many of these
issues myself. But I've also witnessed and experienced the
powerful change that Christ can bring about in a man's
life. For this reason, I'm compelled to expose the problems
and myths, and offer solutions that will bring men back
into fellowship with God and their families to transform
this messed-up culture.

The renowned German author and German psychoana-
lyst Alexander Mitscherlich stated: "Society has torn the
soul of the male, and into this tear the demons have fled
– the demons of insecurity, selfishness, and despair.
Consequently, men do not know who they are as
men. Rather, they define themselves by what they do,

who they know, or by what they own." He wrote these remarks over forty years ago. Can you image what he would say today?

Did you catch that? "Men do not know who they are as men. Rather, they define themselves by what they do, who they know, or by what they own." Authentic manhood has to do with who we *are*, not what we *do*. In other words, authentic manhood is a matter of *being*, not *doing*. I'm not saying that *doing* isn't important, but what we do must come from who we are, and not the other way around.

For example, think about the matter of salvation. We know from Scripture that we are saved by God's grace through faith in Jesus Christ. So, when we place our trust in Christ, we become children of God (the *being* part of the equation). *Being* His children informs us how to live (the *doing* part of the equation).

We don't become children of God by *doing* good things. We *do* good things *because* of who we *are* in Christ, God's children. In the same way, we don't become authentic men by *doing* authentic manhood things. Rather, the authentic man *does* authentic manhood things *because* he is an authentic man.

With the above in mind, let's back up a bit and look at who we are and how an authentic man should view himself. An authentic or biblical or true man is one who recognizes that he was created in God's image. God created us as an earthly expression of Himself, and as such, we exist to glorify God and portray God's image to others.

But the authentic man also recognizes that his own image has been deeply marred by sin. And knowing that there's only one solution for sin – faith in Jesus Christ for the forgiveness of sins – a true man humbles himself before God, repents of his sin, and pursues a growing relationship with Jesus Christ. Through Christ, we put on authentic manhood. We become men of God.

So, knowing Jesus Christ introduces us to authentic manhood, and being an authentic man drives us to want to live like one. Jesus Christ not only serves to usher us into authentic manhood, but He is also our example on how to live authentically. We desperately want to be men who passionately live in service to God and others. But to that end, we also desperately need a godly example to emulate. Who else could qualify as the quintessential authentic man other than our Lord Jesus Christ? Ray Ortlund urges, "Let Jesus be the only hero in your story."

Jesus Is Our Example of Authentic Manhood

Once, when Jesus took Peter, James, and John on a high mountain, the text says, "He was transfigured before them. His face shone like the sun, and His clothes became as white as the light. And behold, Moses and Elijah appeared to them, talking with Him. Then Peter answered and said to Jesus, 'Lord, it is good for us to be here; if You wish, let us make here three

tabernacles: one for You, one for Moses, and one for Elijah'"
(Matthew 17:2-4 NKJV).

Luke's account explains that Peter suggested that "because he didn't know what he was saying"! But while Peter was still speaking, the text says, "Behold, a bright cloud overshadowed them; and suddenly a voice came out of the cloud, saying, 'This is My beloved Son, in whom I am well pleased. Hear Him! [or listen to Him!]'" (Matthew 17:5 NKJV).

This passage powerfully explains what we're getting at here. This was a profound, supernatural experience that Peter, James, and John witnessed. For the first time, they saw Jesus in glorified form speaking with Moses and Elijah. Think about those two Old Testament patriarchs.

Moses led the Children of Israel out of Egypt with great signs and wonders. He led two million Israelites through the wilderness for 40 years. He wrote the first five books of the Bible. God gave Moses the Law. Moses mentored young Joshua to take his place when he died, and Joshua led Israel in the conquest of Canaan.

Then, there was Elijah, a man through whom God did many mighty miracles including raising the dead. Elijah challenged the 450 prophets of the false god Baal. By faith, Elijah won that challenge and proved that the Lord is God. And the Lord loved Elijah so much that He took him to heaven without dying!

It seems like either of those two men would be great examples for us to follow. But what did God say? God interrupted Peter's attempt to take things in hand, and referring to Jesus He said, "This is My beloved Son, in whom I am well pleased. Listen to Him!" Jesus is God's beloved Son. Jesus alone is the one in whom the Father is well pleased. Jesus is the one we are to listen to and follow. Jesus Christ is the one true authentic man. He is our example. We must follow Him and listen to Him. An authentic man is one who follows Jesus. We identify with Him.

Remember, this is how Jesus recruited His disciples: "He said to them, 'Follow Me, and I will make you fishers of men'" (Matthew 4:19 NKJV).

Therefore, authentic manhood describes a man who is following Jesus, the one true authentic man. And because we *are* authentic men in Christ, we listen to Him, we obey Him, we want to be like Him, and we seek to please Him in everything we do. And in following Him, we strive to represent Him well to others. This is how the apostle Paul could say, "Imitate me, just as I also imitate Christ" (NKJV). Or as the New American Standard Version puts it, "Be imitators of me, just as I also am of Christ" (1 Corinthians 11:1).

Discussion Questions:

What issues do you see in your community that are a direct result of the fatherlessness problem?

After reading this chapter what are some changes you would like to make in your life that demonstrate authentic manhood?

By using the many resources on the Men's Ministry Catalyst (MMC) website how can we help you to become a more effective follower of Jesus? www.mensministrycatalyst.org

"A hero is a man who is afraid to run away."
– English proverb

CHAPTER 3

Standing in the Gap for Biblical Manhood

"And the Lord will continually guide you,
And satisfy your desire in scorched places,
And give strength to your bones;
And you will be like a watered garden,
And like a spring of water whose waters do not fail."
– Isaiah 58:11 –

We've consciously chosen the metaphor of a "watchman" and "a man to stand in the gap" for purposes of this book. We've also concluded that a watchman is a man who exhibits authentic manhood and not some sissified, emasculated, passive version like our culture promotes.

You might suspect that at this point we would offer you a long list of rules to keep in order to measure up to true manhood and what God expects of us. But fortunately, Jesus has simplified this for us. When a Pharisee came to Jesus and asked Him, "Teacher, which is the greatest commandment in the Law?" Jesus simply replied, "'You shall love the Lord your God with all your heart, with all your soul, and with all your mind.' This is the first and great commandment. And the second is like it: 'You shall love your neighbor as yourself.' On these two commandments hang all the Law and the Prophets" (Matthew 22:36-39 NKJV).

Long lists of rules to live by offer caveats, loopholes, exceptions, and excuses. Long lists of rules to live by are stifling, discouraging, and impossible to keep. And long lists of rules to live by focus on man's dependence on himself and his ability to keep them, requiring accountability partners to help us toe the line.

Love, on the other hand, knows no caveats, loopholes, exceptions, or excuses. It simply loves to love. Hebrews 12:2 urges us to focus on "Jesus, the originator and perfecter of the faith, who for the joy set before Him endured the cross, … ." We are to be like Jesus who loved us sacrificially "for the joy set before Him." Loving God and loving others is freeing, encouraging, and a delight to pursue. "We love because He first loved us." Loving God and loving others focus on our dependence on God and His infinite, eternal ability to love us and to love through us.

We also know from Scripture that love, like faith, must find expressions to be genuine. "For God so loved the world *that He gave* His only begotten Son." Love is not merely a warm and fuzzy emotion. Love demands and drives action. So, we see that authentic or biblical manhood is quite radical in its approach to life compared with the focus of our culture today.

Love God with all your being and love others like you love yourself. That's it! An authentic man loves God and loves others with all the fervency, intensity, courage, and strength he can muster. He doesn't waver. He never shrinks from his calling. He doesn't lose sight of his purpose. He is faithful to his Lord, his wife and family, and others.

Love for his Lord motivates him to strive to be more like Jesus in every way whether in the home as a husband and father, or at work as a boss or employee, or in his church, or in his neighborhood. In all he does, the authentic man seeks to please his Lord out of deep love and devotion for Him.

Love for his wife and children motivates the authentic man to serve, protect, and provide for his family, always putting their needs above his own. He serves as their watchman. He stands in the gap for them. He does this willingly and joyfully as expressions of his great love for them and for His Lord. The biblical man is present with his family both physically and emotionally out of his desire to lead them and demonstrate for them what it means to love the Lord and to love each other.

The authentic man looks to Jesus as his chief example in order to provide his family with an example of what it means to follow Jesus. But just like Adam, the silence of many good men may look like approval of what contemporary society promotes. God seeks motivated and loving men, who will take a stand for what is right. We must lovingly but boldly speak truth and grace to everyone.

Friends, we have a war going on that is as equally devastating as if nuclear bombs were being dropped on our country. Men must rise up and become warriors and watchmen for God and their families or this culture is doomed; our families are doomed. We must adopt an agenda of love, hope, strength, courage, and great character for the younger generation.

We've defined authentic or biblical manhood as a man who intensely loves His Lord and others, especially his wife and children. And we have concluded that genuine love, like faith, must express itself in action.

This is super important because when we hear the term "watchman" used today, our minds may turn to the image of a soldier standing guard. The problem with this image is that unless there is an attack, the soldier standing guard seems passive. But passivity is far from what this image should portray!

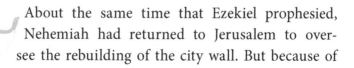

About the same time that Ezekiel prophesied, Nehemiah had returned to Jerusalem to oversee the rebuilding of the city wall. But because of opposition from their enemies, Nehemiah put all the men on alert. In fact, we read, "Those who were rebuilding the wall and those who carried burdens carried with one hand doing the work, and the other keeping hold of a weapon. As for the builders, each wore his sword strapped to his waist as he built, while [a]the trumpeter stood near me" (Nehemiah 4:17-18).

In this context, the watchman's duty was one of vigilance, looking to defend the city, but it was by no means passive. These men were not only standing in the gap, but they were *closing* the gaps in the wall to prevent future enemy attacks. They held their weapons in one hand and their tools in the other. This serves as a great image for us as well.

You might be wondering: What are *our* tools and weapons?

In Ephesians 6:10-18, the apostle Paul gives us the answer to that question. So, in this chapter and in the remainder of this book, we're going to inspect the tools and weapons that the Lord has given us to do battle for our families. These are the tools and weapons with which we can build strong families, serve as watchmen for them, and provide them with a godly example to follow.

But before we walk through the Lord's armory of weapons and tools, Paul is keen to get our heads and hearts in the right place. This is crucial, because a soldier can be fully equipped and outfitted, but if his head and heart aren't where they should be, his weapons will do him no good.

I love the powerful images portrayed in the epic battles in *The Lord of the Rings* movie series. Two specific battle speeches come to mind: the first was King Thoren's and the second was Aragorn's. As you listen to their rallying cries before their men and hear the rattling of sabers and lances you can feel yourself preparing for a courageous battle against the forces of evil. You see men muster great courage despite their fear of what they're about to face.

In a similar way, Paul begins his battle cry in Ephesians 6:10 (NKJV), "Finally, my brethren, be strong in the Lord and in the power of His might. Put on the whole armor of God, that you may be able to stand against the wiles of the devil. For we do not wrestle against flesh and blood, but against principalities, against powers, against the rulers of the darkness of this age, against spiritual hosts of wickedness in the heavenly places."

Paul reminds us that this is no ordinary battle. We're not fighting against people. It's not a "flesh-and-blood" struggle. We're engaging in warfare with the devil himself and against his evil minions. We desperately need this reminder, or we're doomed! We dare not try to enter this fight in our own strength.

Just to be clear, our enemy is not a particular political party or other human entity. Our enemy isn't people for whom Christ died – even if they currently stand in defiance to Him. Our enemy is none other than Satan himself and the powers of darkness. For it is Satan who has deceived people and is holding them captive to do his will.

In and of ourselves, we do not possess the strength or power to fight against this supernatural enemy. That's why Paul begins this passage the way he does, "Finally, my brethren, be strong in the Lord and in the power of His might." We must fight this battle in the strength and power of the Lord. He enables us to stand against the devil.

But how do we do this? How do we grasp the Lord's strength? How do we avail ourselves of His mighty power? We do so by faith. That's the only way.

Earlier in Paul's letter to the church in Ephesus, he prayed the following prayer for them. Please read this text carefully and imagine that Paul was praying this prayer over you:

> Therefore I also, after I heard of your faith in the Lord Jesus and your love for all the saints, do not cease to give thanks for you, making mention of you in my prayers: that the God of our Lord Jesus Christ, the Father of glory, may give to you the spirit of wisdom and revelation in the knowledge of Him, the eyes of your understanding being enlightened; that you may know what is the hope of His calling, what are the riches of the glory of His inheritance in the saints, and what is *the exceeding greatness of His power toward us who believe,* according to the working of *His mighty*

power which He worked in Christ when He raised Him from the dead and seated Him at His right hand in the heavenly places, far above all *principality* and *power* and *might* and *dominion*, and every name that is named, not only in this age but also in that which is to come. And He put all things under His feet and gave Him to be head over all things to the church, which is His body, the fullness of Him who fills all in all. (Ephesians 1:15-23 NKJV emphasis mine)

The Scriptures declare, "For whatever things were written before were written for our learning, that we through the patience and comfort of the Scriptures might have hope" (Romans 15:4 NKJV). So, the passage above was not only Paul's prayer for the Ephesian believers, but we know that the Lord wants us to apply this prayer to ourselves as well. So, let's look a bit more closely at what the Lord wants for us.

He wants to give us the spirit of wisdom and revelation in the knowledge of Him (i.e., in our relationship with Him). In other words, the Lord Himself wants to give us more and more wisdom and insight into who He is so that we might continually be on a track to knowing Him better. He wants to open our eyes to see and understand all that He has prepared for us, both in this life and in eternity. We must not be deceived by thinking that what the world has to offer is all there is. The riches He speaks of are "the riches of His glory."

An advancing army cannot hope to engage successfully in battle without a constant flow of supplies and resources to outfit its soldiers. The Lord's supply is limitless and readily available. He also wants us to grasp "the exceeding greatness of His power toward us who believe." This is the same power with which He raised the Lord Jesus from the dead. So, the power He makes available to us is limitless!

Finally, Jesus is our Commander-and-Chief. We are subject to Him. We look to Him for our marching orders. He provides the intel and strategy for the battle. It's also plain from the passage that He works through His church. This assures us that we are not alone in the battle, nor should we strike out on our own. We are comrades in arms with other brothers in Christ.

This then, is how we stand in the gap for biblical manhood – by loving Christ and others with our whole being, and by arming ourselves with spiritual weapons and strength that only the Lord can provide.

Discussion Questions:

How do you see your role as a "watchman" for your family, community, and church?

What other men do you know and look up to as watchmen who exemplify biblical manhood? What are some ways you can partner with them to fortify your own resolve and character?

Look again at the spiritual weapons Paul lists in Ephesians 6:10-18. Where do you see yourself lacking? How will you respond to this need in your life?

"Everyone has an earthly father. Some fathers are absent or are not positive role models – but God's original design was to have the father as the leader of the family. Whether your father was a godly leader or not, you can always look to God the Father as the ultimate example."

– Pastor Jack Wellman

CHAPTER 4

Standing in the Gap for Your Family

So then, while we have opportunity,
let's do good to all people, and especially to those who are of
the household of the faith.

– Galatians 6:10 –

In the introduction of this book, I mentioned some of the heroes of my childhood. What kid in their dreams didn't want to be someone like Superman? I fantasized about being a strong man who could help save the world or at least another person in distress. Do you know a person who "stands in the gap" for others and takes on difficult challenges like Superman does for people in trouble?

As an aging man I still have that passion of being a watchman for others. It is normal for me to run towards action and danger. That predisposition has helped me in my capacity as a chaplain with police and fire departments.

Until the "Woke People" got involved, most little boys had a natural bent towards being rescuers, warriors, and defenders. Despite the pressures of our culture, I believe many young men today are drawn to join things like the Boy Scouts, the military, or an occupation that has some risk associated with it. And some men today are looking for a mentor who could help teach them how to be a strong man with a clear vision for their future.

God has given men the innate desire to take on the responsibility and headship of their home serving as rescuers and protectors of their families. Just like the captain of a ship is responsible for setting a correct course and giving the proper commands for his crew members, in the same way a man is to lead in the home. Psychologists tell us that children who know that their dads pray for them every day and help direct them spiritually enjoy a deep sense of love and security.

Men who try to make a difference and set an example and direction for the family to follow are vital to the health of the family. We are to be conquers, victors, and advocates for justice and biblical truth, and who hold evil doers at bay and keep them from entering our homes. I appreciate the masterful work of Dr. Tony Evans in his book *Kingdom Men* (a.k.a., Watchmen) however, I do not support some of his more recent drifts toward wokeism and ideas that could be contrary to Scripture. Having said that, we can agree with this powerful comment about men:

> When a kingdom man steps out his door each day, heaven, earth, and hell take notice. When he protects the woman under his care, she can do little to resist him. His children look to him with confidence. Other men look to him as someone to emulate. His church calls on him for strength and leadership. He is a preserver of culture and a champion of society to keep out evil and usher in good. A kingdom man understands that God never said a godly life would be easy, He just said it would be worth it. [7]

I didn't have many men in my life when I was young who modeled biblical manhood. But God's Word drew me in, and I was fascinated with exploring the heroes of the faith who modeled what it means to be a true watchman

---

7   Tony Evans, *Kingdom Man: Every Man's Destiny, Every Woman's Dream* (Carol Stream, Illinois: Tyndale House Publisher, Inc., 2015) Introduction.

(protector, hero, rescuer) for our nation, families, and those under our care.

I learned that a godly man is like the watchman for his family. He is to "stand in the gap" for his tribe as a defender of truth and a strong protector. Metaphorically speaking, a watchman is to stand in the gap to slay the dragons of life that seek to attack the family: dragons of immorality, indecency, false teachings, and bad behavior that are threatening our families, communities, and the church.

A family watchman exemplifies the Kingdom of God to his family. He doesn't allow the influences of the world to distract his family from the Word of God or from the rule of God in their lives.

Where Does This Phrase "Stand in the Gap" Come From?

The words "stand in the gap" appear in Ezekiel 22:30. After King David's reign, the kings in Israel had become progressively more wicked, leading their people into grievous sexual sins and idolatry, even to the point of offering their children in sacrifice to false gods. The kingdom of Israel had been split in two: Israel to the north and Judah to the south.

Israel to the north forsook the Lord completely, so the Lord sent Assyria to conquer Israel and carry them into exile. Then, some years later, He used Nebuchadnezzar King of Babylon to destroy Judah and exile them to Babylon. Nebuchadnezzar carried off Judah's King

Jehoiachin and appointed his uncle Zedekiah, as king in his place. But the Jews continued to sin grievously under Zedekiah's rule.

In the ninth year of Zedekiah's reign, he rebelled against Nebuchadnezzar. So, Nebuchadnezzar marched against Jerusalem again to put down this insurrection. This time, Nebuchadnezzar utterly destroyed the city. Ezekiel was among the exiles from Judah in Babylon when he received God's words for the people. And it was leading up to the destruction of Jerusalem that the Lord told Ezekiel, "I looked for someone among them who would build up the wall and stand before me in the gap on behalf of the land so I would not have to destroy it, but I found no one." So, Jerusalem was destroyed. This is truly one of the most tragic accounts in the Bible!

The Lord placed His Spirit within Ezekiel and called him to be such a man to stand in the gap on behalf of his people (Ezekiel 2:1-7). The Lord told Ezekiel, "Son of man, I have appointed you as a watchman for the house of Israel; whenever you hear a word from My mouth, warn them from Me" (Ezekiel 3:17).

And so, it is today with us. God is looking for men who will stand in the gap as watchmen for their families and nation. He is looking for an Abraham who stood in the gap for Sodom. He is looking for a Moses who pled on behalf of Israel. He is looking for an Ezekiel who spoke God's words to the rebellious exiles. But just like God did in the Old Testament – without men who will stand in the gap – the Lord will bring judgment upon our nation.

What Does it Mean to "Stand in the Gap"?

While the phrase "stand in the gap" only occurs once in Scripture, there are numerous examples of men who stood in the gap on behalf of others. For instance, Moses "stood in the gap" and pled with God not to destroy the Children of Israel when they made a golden calf and declared it to be their god (Exodus 32:9-11).

In biblical times, cities had walls built around them to protect them from attack. The wall and those who guarded it (the watchman) were symbols of strength and security. The city's inhabitants felt a degree of safety when the wall was fortified, and the watchmen were keeping watch.

If the wall of a city was breached during a siege, defenders would swarm to the breach to protect the citizens of the village. As soon as possible, they sought to repair the breach and fortify it against future breaks. A breach in the wall that was not repaired or defended would mean the city could fall. Every resident was responsible for reporting a breach in front of their home and trying to repair it as soon as possible.

During the time of Isaiah, Ezekiel, Jeremiah, and Nehemiah, God's people had a "breach" in the "wall" of their lives. They had let down their guard, and through pride and disobedience, their lives had been breached. Sin crept in and began to reign in their lives. Most people were so caught up in sin that they left no room to pursue the Lord. They were disobedient and careless toward the Law and their covenant relationship with God because of their idolatry. As a result, Psalm 78:62 declares that God, "... also turned His people over to the sword, and was filled with wrath at His inheritance."

When Ezekiel shared the words God spoke to him, he told the people that God was prepared to send down His wrath and destroy Jerusalem because of their sin and rebellion. Judgment was coming. As we ponder God's Word and look at the sin and spiritual void of our nation, the warnings and words of our Lord once again are a clarion call for us to turn from our ways and seek His forgiveness.

A Clarion Call for Today

In the modern world, we do not have literal walls surrounding our cities. The walls we do have or have had are spiritual walls. David recognized this spiritual application when he wrote, "The Lord is my rock and my fortress and my savior, My God, my rock, in whom I take refuge; My shield and the horn of my salvation, my stronghold" (Psalm 18:2). The breaches in our spiritual wall that we experience are the result of our lack of trust in the Lord and our disobedience to Him. And through these breaches all manner of sin threatens or has already infiltrated our lives and those of our families.

When we stand in the gap for our family or others, we are urging them to trust the Lord and live fully for Him. And we are asking God to help them when they cannot help themselves. We are asking God to protect, care, and assist others when all seems lost.

When we stand in the gap, we are working to accomplish God's will for His people. No Christian wants to see others hurt, frightened, or hopeless. We desire, like God, to see people come to know the saving grace of our Lord. We don't want anyone to spend eternity in hell. Consequently, we must patch the breaches in the walls of our family and nation while being vigilant against future attacks.

Standing in the gap as a watchman is like a shepherd watching over his sheep. We must stay alert, awake, and courageous even when a bear, a wolf, or a lion threatens them. As watchmen we stand for the truth and we're vigilant to guard against the lies and deception so rampant in our culture.

Standing in the Gap as a Father – The Family Watchman

Christ is the head of the Church. "He is also the head of the body, the church; and He is the beginning, the firstborn from the dead, so that He Himself will come to have first place in everything" (Colossians 1:18). "And He put all things in subjection under His feet, and made Him head over all things to the church,

which is His body, the fullness of Him who fills all in all."
(Ephesians 1:22-23)

In a similar manner, the man represents Christ in the
home. Christ has given him the headship for his family. He
is to take on the responsibilities of leadership while shep-
herding his family's spiritual growth. But Paul clarifies,
"... I want you to understand that Christ is the head of every man, and the man is the head of a woman, and God is
the head of Christ" (1 Corinthians 11:3).

The man of the family has a spiritual role as a family pastor, shepherd, mediator, leader, discipler, and wise coun-
selor. He leads his family members through God's Word,
prayer, meditation, the power of the Holy Spirit, and
through mature Christians within his church and among
his acquaintances.

Seven Ways We Can Stand in the Gap for Our Family

In identifying some of the ways a man can stand in the
gap for his family there is so much more we could say. So, I
recommend that you study these points further with other
resources to dig deeper into the truths listed below.

Take on the Spiritual Leadership

When families face hardships, challenges, or despair, the
family looks to their parents, and especially dad,
for wisdom, reassurance, hope, and encouragement. If a father reveres and submits to God in all

things, his faith will be a source of comfort for his family members and help them feel secure, regardless of what the storms of life bring against them.

King Solomon asserted, "In the fear of the Lord there is strong confidence, and his children will have refuge" (Proverbs 14:26). In this chaotic world where direct communication with family members is hijacked by cell phones and computers, we must work extra hard to engage face-to-face with those we love.

Spiritual leadership is a learned discipline that comes with the responsibility to be proactive in the lives of one's family. It can be a difficult tightrope to walk when teenage children are involved. You want them to become independent and learn how to make good decisions, but you don't want them to walk away from biblical teachings and sound judgment. My wife and I found one of the best ways to help cultivate these attributes is to encourage our children to be around other families that share our values and embrace healthy communications.

Be an Encourager

The words of a father are powerful. They can either do great harm or great good. A father's words can either crush a child's spirit or build their confidence and trust.

The apostle Paul underscores some ways fathers love and lead their children: through encouragement, comfort, and steadfastly reminding them to live in a way that glorifies God. Perhaps he learned this through his mentor, Barnabas, whose name means "son of encouragement" (Acts 4:36).

The writer of Hebrews reminds us "… let's consider how to encourage one another in love and good deeds" (Hebrews 10:24). The unique relationship between father and child creates many opportunities to do this.

To this father, grandfather, and now great grandfather, the seven most important words I can tell our children to exhort and comfort them is "I'm proud of you and I love you!" Isn't that what Paul told the believers in Thessalonica, "just as you know how we were exhorting and encouraging and imploring each one of you as a father would his own children, so that you would walk in a manner worthy of the God who calls you into His own kingdom and glory" (1 Thessalonians 2:11-12).

Intercessory Prayer

My wife and I consider praying for our family members the most important thing we can do for them. As our Heavenly Father gives good things to us, His children, so an earthly father desires to provide good things for his family (Matthew 7:9-11). Jesus uses this example to remind us that God is a much better father than any human could ever be. As His children, we can trust God to provide us with good things.

A wise father knows the gifts and attention that his family needs, and he endeavors to supply those within his means. And conversely, a wise father protects his family from things that distract them from the Lord and pursuing Him. This wisdom and enabling comes from God's Holy Spirit within us. He teaches us and leads us through prayer and His Word.

> Now in the same way the Spirit also helps our weakness; for we do not know what to pray for as we should, but the Spirit Himself intercedes for us with groanings too deep for words; and He who searches the hearts knows what the mind of the Spirit is, because He intercedes for the saints according to the will of God.
>
> And we know that God causes all things to work together for good to those who love God, to those who are called according to His purpose. (Romans 8:26-28)

Model a Servant's Heart

When a father shows generosity to others or lends a helping hand, he is modeling Christ's love and kindness. He projects to his family, "I'm not going to be selfish. I'm going to help someone out who may be struggling with his or her life." When we help someone in need, we give them a chance to reboot or take a step back to better assess their issues. You also are sharing the love of God with them. Making this a family project helps bring the family together in a special way.

There are people all around us that need a helping hand. When someone is struggling in your community, pray as a family about how your tribe can help and then act on God's instruction. This will help your children understand God's command to love others.

We were blessed to have twin sons who were given an amazing gift of music very young in life. They use this gift in a variety of ways including writing, arranging, conducting, and performing. They used their gifts in assisting our ministry with worship during many conferences, family retreats, pastors training sessions, and a host of other programs.

When the boys were about twelve and putting on paid performances, we discussed how they could use their gifts to inspire and encourage those less fortunate. We decided to tour three rest homes after our family Christmas morning celebration of gift opening and brunch. The boys performed some of their favorite Christmas songs along with some original pieces. The senior audience, many of them shut-ins with no family around, were absolutely overjoyed.

Our sons learned a lesson about having a servant's heart and representing Christ's love to others. To this day they continue to use their talents as worship leaders and pastors.

Be Transparent and Honest

In our family one of the character traits we most cherished was honesty. Regardless of the circumstances, we did not tolerate lying. That applied to my wife and me as well. As parents we wish not to admit failures and weaknesses in front of others, much less in front of our children. One way to encourage your children to respect you is to admit your failures and ask for their forgiveness when appropriate.

Let's get the matter of respect straight right now. The fifth of the Ten Commandments instructs us to honor our parents. That is the children's responsibility. But the subtle responsibility behind it for the parents is to bring them up in a way that makes honoring us easy. Obviously, we all sin and make mistakes rearing our children. In view of our frailty, we aren't worthy of their respect. But the Lord has given us authority over our children, and we are responsible to love and care for them, bringing them up in the nurture and admonition of the Lord. So, when we are real with our kids, they will respect us MORE, not less.

When we humble ourselves before our child and admit a mistake or sin, they will be more apt to own up to their mistakes and sin as well. This one thing draws them to Christ more than anything else. It makes the Christian walk real and possible, instead of putting it on a pedestal they can never reach.

King Solomon's wisdom once again gives us guidance:

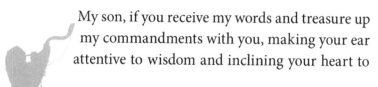

My son, if you receive my words and treasure up my commandments with you, making your ear attentive to wisdom and inclining your heart to understanding; yes, if you call out for insight and raise your voice for understanding, if you seek it like silver and search for it as for hidden treasures, then you will understand the fear of the Lord and find the knowledge of God. (Proverbs 2:1-5 ESV)

The apostle Paul also urged Timothy, "Do your best to present yourself to God as one approved, a worker who has no need to be ashamed, rightly handling the word of truth" (2 Timothy 2:15 ESV).

It may seem strange to discuss a personal characteristic like transparency when talking about standing in the gap for others, but it is important. Standing in the gap for others can only happen when we are transparent and honest. But if we lack integrity and are posing as something we are not, then how can we claim we have a good relationship with God, much less stand in the gap on behalf of others?

Author Brené Brown said:

If we want greater clarity in our purpose or deeper, and more meaningful spiritual lives, vulnerability is the path. We cannot hold anything back from God. To be vulnerable is to allow yourself to be seen: heart, soul, and mind. We find our deeper purpose when we lay everything at the foot of the cross. There will be nothing clouding our discernment of God's plan for our lives.[8]

Problem Solving and Conflict Resolution

Coming from an educational and career background, it was easy to fall into the role of trying to be the "answer man" as questions and conflicts arose in our home. Consequently, I did a poor job of giving our sons and my wife the opportunity to fail and become accountable for their own mistakes. In retrospect it would have been better to let them fail more and suffer the consequences of poor decision making, than to always bail them out. It would have also been a good idea to teach them the approach on how to make good decisions rather than feed them the answers.

As a child I didn't have adult role models who modeled how to go about making good decisions. Mine was the school of "hard knocks" resulting in some lost opportunities, financial mistakes, and other bad choices. Consequently, my zeal to be an involved father in the lives of my family may have stifled their ability to resolve conflicts and make tough decisions on their own.

When we don't know the answer to help in decision making a good watchman will say, "I don't know, but let's discover

---

8 Brené Brown, Ph.D., *Daring Greatly: How the Courage to Be Vulnerable Transforms the Way We Live, Love, Parent, and Lead* (New York: Penguin Random House, 2015).

ways to find the answer together." Or we can ask, "What do you think you should do in this situation?"

Avoiding conflict is natural for most of us. The key to conflict resolution is being able to see and respect another person's ideas and convictions. Conflict can actually help us affirm our own convictions and lead us to discover other avenues to the solution of a problem. And in resolving differences, we want to avoid blaming others, embarrassing them, or frustrating them.

When your kids have questions, problems, concerns, or even just need a reminder, open the Bible for answers and talk through it. Show them how to research an answer. Show them how to use a Bible concordance. And show them how to simply open the Bible and pray Scripture they know, even if it doesn't apply to their exact situation. All these approaches lead to hearing more truth, which will always lead us down the right path because God promises it will (Proverbs 3:5-6)!

Family Devotions

If you are having a family devotion or worship time at all, I want you to know how thrilled I am. I say that not because you need to impress me or anything, but because I know personally how hard it is to make this happen. So, I'm hesitant to mess with whatever you're doing but bear with me. I pray it helps rather than frustrates or overwhelms.

Most people have a devotion time where they read a portion of a book (or even the Bible), pray, and then call it good. It's not enough. I would argue that the most important part of your time together as a family is the discussion about what you read. Take time to do this, even if it means you read less, it will benefit your family more.

When our sons were at home, the evening devotion time around the dinner table might include time dedicated to the discussion of what God was teaching us in our quiet times. In those situations, we didn't necessarily read the Bible together. Instead, our time focused on applying what we read on our own and sharing that with each other. Of course, we do read the Bible together at other times, but the evening was reserved for this format.

We would take one evening a week and devote it towards family discussions of biblical themes and mix in some fun games or adventures that helped the kids look forward to the night. Maybe it was as simple as roasting hot dogs in a fire pit or doing a trust walk with your eyes closed in the back yard. Whatever we did was fun for all of us as we drew closer to one another.

Final Thoughts

While it is important to make margin for failure and help your children develop good problem-solving skills, it is ultimately the responsibility of the father to be the gate keeper. The family needs to know that when tough things come, and danger is lurking around the corner the words from dad need to be "I've got this" or "It's on me."

Whether the man of the house handles the problem directly or seeks a solution to the problem from other godly men, the family knows that dad is going to be the ultimate guide, shepherd, defender, and rescuer. This truth places the weight of untangling serious issues where it biblically belongs – on the family's watchman who stands in the gap for family values.

Discussion Questions

What new revelations about your role as the "family gate keeper" has this chapter brought to mind?

How might you implement the seven ways for standing in the gap for your family?

Given the crazy presence of social media and scrambled news reporting how might you help your family create a godly perspective on life and problem solving?

"Light brings illumination into the darkness.
Light brightens up our lives. Light above all permits us to
see and to discern. The Christian in the public square must
be one who knows how to discern and not just discern on
individual issues but discern about the deeper
dimensions of being a person and to lead others on this
same process of discernment."
– Diarmuid Martin Archbishop of Dublin

CHAPTER 5

Standing in the Gap in the Marketplace

"For as the body without the spirit is dead, so faith without
works is dead also."
– James 2:26 NKJV –

In biblical times the watchmen were stationed on the wall
of the city, alert to any danger that might approach
the city. The city walls provided protection against

attack and especially at night-time when it might be easiest for an enemy to try to sneak in.

The walls were not meant to isolate people and keep them from interacting with the world outside the city. They had their business, trading, and trips that took them to areas far away from the city. As they passed through one of the many gates located around the wall it would have been a comfort to see a watchman on duty ensuring the safety of the city.

The gates provided a place where people could meet and talk over the issues surrounding their lives. Political, social, and religious conversations were common topics you would experience when passing through the gates. The watchmen would have been privy to these conversations.

I think of those ancient city walls as analogous to our church campuses today. But instead of venturing out, most church leaders rarely leave the confines of their campuses. Too many pastors believe that ministry happens best in the controlled environment of their church and that missionaries or para-church organizations are best equipped to minister to people in the public square or marketplace away from the church.

Some pastors believe that their conservative congregation risks contamination from the world if they are too exposed or involved in the public square. I do appreciate this concern some pastors have. After all, there are those more liberal pastors and churches who actively support the crazy deviations from biblical values that lean into Woke values. These liberal pastors are the ones you see most in the public square and on news reports. They have given the rest of us who wish to minister in the public square cause to pause about our involvement because we might be viewed as belonging to one of the radical social movements.

The radical pastors who accept the unbiblical models of social movements are prostituting their liturgical collars for the sake of personal exposure. A few pastors have even been financially supported by political campaigns as part of their agreement to participate. The movement has become a religion in itself. These are the ever-changing social and political agendas that are not a part of traditional Christian values.

Having said all that, however, does not excuse us from getting out into the world to represent Christ well to the lost.

A Biblical Perspective on the Gates and Courtyards

Throughout Scripture we see how the public square was used as a gathering place for interaction, debate, inspiration, and equipping.

In the book of Ezra, we read:

> And all the people gathered as one man into the square before the Water Gate. And they told Ezra the scribe to bring the Book of the Law of

Moses that the Lord had commanded Israel. So, Ezra the priest brought the Law before the assembly, both men and women and all who could understand what they heard, on the first day of the seventh month. And he read from it facing the square before the Water Gate from early morning until midday, in the presence of the men and the women and those who could understand. And the ears of all the people were attentive to the Book of the Law. (Nehemiah 8:1-3 ESV)

Nehemiah used the public square to rally the people to work on building the walls of the city. In Genesis the angels met Lot in the gateway of the city and when he invited them to stay with him, they said they would spend the night in the square. (Genesis19:2) The public square was a place for travelers to camp out. Such was the case in Judges 19:15 when a Levite was without a room and found himself meeting a new friend in the city square.

Finally, we see a strong case for evangelism in the public square in Acts 17:17, "So he [Paul] was reasoning in the synagogue with the Jews and the God-fearing Gentiles, and in the marketplace every day with those who happened to be present."

A Public Square Ministry

In Matthew 28 Jesus tells us to "go make disciples" of all nations. As I reread that chapter, I'm convinced He was telling us to get out into the world and meet people where they are. In fact, in the original Greek, the word "go" is a participle, not an active verb. The active verb in Jesus' command is to "make disciples." So, the word "go" is better rendered "going." Therefore, we can understand what Jesus was saying, "As you are going through life, make disciples."

To be involved in the public square is not necessarily being a political activist but being "salt and light" to this corrupt world. It is to represent Christ Jesus and His teaching to a lost world. Salt loses its power if left in the saltshaker (a.k.a., the church building). Yes, we need to come together to worship, hear the Word, pray together, and fellowship, but following Jesus also means that we are out in the world (the marketplace) telling others about Him.

Jesus was firm about this point:

> You are the salt of the earth, but if salt has lost its taste, how shall its saltiness be restored? It is no longer good for anything except to be thrown out and trampled under people's feet.

> You are the light of the world. A city set on a hill cannot be hidden. Nor do people light a lamp and put it under a basket, but on a stand, and it gives light to all in the house. In the same way, let

your light shine before others, so that they may see
your good works and give glory to your Father who
is in heaven. (Matthew 5:13-16 ESV)

It is interesting to note that most of Christ's ministry was
outside the temple. It was ministry in the public square.
Most of His miracles were done in the marketplace, or outside either the temple or a synagogue.

Taking God's Word to the World

The primary mission of Men's Ministry Catalyst (MMC)
is to share with pastors and lay-leaders the importance of
developing vibrant and dynamic ministries to men that
help them in their spiritual journeys. God has equipped
MMC with various Scripture-proven practices, resources,
and program models that inspire men and help equip them
for service within the church and their communities.

In the early years of our ministry, we endeavored to meet
with several pastors around California. We believe strongly
in the local church and the importance of regularly partici-
pating in a church focused on God's Word and discipleship.

But few pastors desired to launch evangelistic opportunities that brought their ministries to the people in the public square. Instead, they told me, "I'm interested in your
ministry only if you can bring more people to my
Sunday Service."

Given the limited support among several pastors, Let's Go Fishing Ministry (a.k.a. Men's Ministry Catalyst) launched our ministry at Christian Conference Centers, Sports Shows, Tackle Industry Conventions, Fairs, and anywhere we could engage with unsaved people. Through the grace of God opening doors and the support of prominent Christian outdoorsmen, we became a ministry with national influence that was known to millions of outdoorsmen who might not have otherwise received an invitation to know Jesus Christ.

Platforms were opened to us on television, radio, business forums, and professional sports teams all because we began by meeting their perceived needs (learning to fish, fly cast, hunt, or develop family values by building memories in the outdoors). The outdoors was originally our "public square" that God provided to open the doors of opportunity to thousands of churches around the world. Many pastors eventually saw the fruit of being in the marketplace and working outside the walls of the church campus.

Thousands who accepted Jesus at a Christian conference center, at a prayer breakfast, at a fishing or hunting show, or who attended one of our many clinics and family camps ultimately ended up going to a good Bible believing church.

Church growth happened and men's ministry programs began to thrive because of the involvement in the public square. Many men could see the benefit of using their passion for the outdoors as a way to reach others with the Gospel. Since 1981 MMC has been assisting churches in building their ministry to men and we are still attracted to the public square.

During the past few years, we recognized that many men attending the churches we were involved with were AWOL in the summer. Where were they? Many could be found enjoying various lakes, rivers, and streams. Some were enjoying picnics, hikes, and retreats to the mountains.

We recognized that many people in the Inland Northwest enjoy the abundant water resources and the recreation that it offers during the summer. We decided to try an experimental program that would meet unchurched people where they were – on the lakes and rivers.

We started a Church on the Water program near the very large Pend Oreille Lake in Northern Idaho. We put the word out and people came by boat, jet ski, or on foot from a neighboring camp area to a very simple worship service on the water. With a public address system, some guitar music, and a clear biblical message, we saw a weekly crowd of about 50-60 people.

From that ten-week, three-year program we ultimately saw over 45 people accept Jesus as their personal Savior. From that group about 17 asked to be baptized in the river where we held the service. Almost all the people ended up taking one of our free Bibles or other resources. Most of those who came to Christ connected with a local church where they are now faithfully attending services.

Get Involved in the Marketplace

God is intensely interested in this world of human social engagement and activity where we spend most of our time. The Bible clearly and comprehensively attests to this in both Testaments.

Jesus, Paul, and Peter regularly used the marketplace (gates and public squares) as a place to present their messages. People did try to shut them down, but that did not stop them from spreading the Gospel.

Jesus prayed over His disciples and ultimately over us:

> "I have given them your word, and the world has hated them because they are not of the world, just as I am not of the world. I do not ask that you take them out of the world, but that you keep them from the evil one. They are not of the world, just as I am not of the world. Sanctify them in the truth; your word is truth. As you sent me into the world, so I have sent them into the world. And for their sake I consecrate myself, that they also may be sanctified in truth. (John 17:14-19 ESV)

Paul told us to be in the world but not let the world contaminate us. "And do not be conformed to this world, but be transformed by the renewing of your mind, so that you may prove what the will of God is, that which is good and acceptable and perfect" (Romans 12:2).

In this country and in the 21ˢᵗ century, the concept of the marketplace has expanded to electronic and virtual forms on the Internet. But unfortunately, some are trying to restrict the marketplace for their messages only. They stifle and censor the message of Christ and seek to eliminate it from public discourse altogether.

The vast majority of "internet platforms" are filtered and controlled by the ungodly who wish to abuse and disrespect evangelical Christians by limiting our access and presence in the public square. The media and many large corporations believe the Christian theology isn't supportive or inclusive enough to their corrupt lifestyles and behaviors. We are called "racist" and "intolerant" by people who don't care enough to understand that our faith is about love, forgiveness, and inclusion.

Undoubtedly, by writing this book, some will criticize and mock me because they cannot wrap their minds around having a person speak biblical truth and challenge their ungodly thinking. But of course, Jesus warned us this would happen, and the apostles joined in with the warning. Paul wrote, "Indeed, all who want to live in a godly way in Christ Jesus will be persecuted" (2 Timothy 3:12).

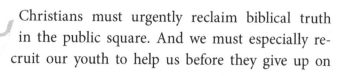

Christians must urgently reclaim biblical truth in the public square. And we must especially recruit our youth to help us before they give up on

Christianity entirely. We must renounce Christianity's unfaithful past in America and those who still embrace it and demonstrate true biblical Christianity. And we must prepare youth to embody Christianity in ways that lead to social change.

Most people under 40 years of age are very skilled at using social media to communicate their ideas and feelings. We should tap into their energy and abilities and help bring people back into a biblical mindset so they can defend the faith and our freedoms well in the marketplace. We need men to stand in the gap and avail themselves of the amazing tools and resources in the marketplace before us.

Discussion Questions:

Until the advent of the Internet, it was hard to imagine how our Lord's command to take the Gospel into all the world could be accomplished. How could you use modern technology to reach others for Jesus? What about passing along the Weekly Devotionals provided by Men's Ministry Catalyst at *www.mensministrycatalyst.org/devotionals?*

How can you encourage your church to get involved in the marketplace? (Some ideas might include attending school board meetings, city council meetings, and becoming involved in service organizations.)

Define your personal "marketplace." Who and what does it encompass? What opportunities do you currently have to represent Christ in your marketplace? What are some ways you could expand your marketplace? What are your biggest challenges in representing Christ in your marketplace?

What can you do with the technology you use every day to stand in the gap for biblical truth and to counter the lies, distortions, and ideas of the "counterculture advocates" who are promoting hopelessness and despair?

There is no assurance like the Word of God. Every word of God is true. God is the truth. There is nothing like the Word of God, a living water, that never runs dry.

CHAPTER 6

Standing in the Gap Before the Lord

"I searched for a man among them who would build up a wall and stand in the gap before Me for the land, so that I would not destroy it; but I found no one."
– Ezekiel 22:30 –

The above quote from the Lord in Ezekiel is both chilling and convicting. The nation of Israel had become exceedingly sinful. In that chapter, the Lord enumerates their sins: the shedding of blood, all manner of sexual sins (adultery, sodomy, fornication, incest, sexual abuse, and assault), taking bribes, extortion, oppressing the poor, denying justice to foreigners, wicked leaders, and the list goes on.

Israel had truly degenerated to the level of a wicked nation that had forgotten God and reveled in the debauchery of evil. This created a cleft, a chasm, a huge gap between them and the Lord. And this people had become so thoroughly debased, that as the Lord searched for someone to intercede on behalf of Israel, call them to repentance, and fill that gap, He found no one. Let that sink in.

Look over that list of sins again and tell me you don't see the same evil in our own country today. Our nation and its leaders call good evil, and evil good. They not only accept evil but promote and even celebrate it! Even many of our churches have bought into lies and deception. Our nation is polluted with the innocent blood of tens of millions of the unborn, and some states are pushing for infanticide. I fear that our list of sins already exceeds that of ancient Israel.

The California Governor has applauded billboards being placed at the gateways of the Golden State telling women to come to California and get their abortions. Can you imagine promoting and flaunting the murder of innocent unborn children and calling it something good?

What are we to do?

Will You Stand in the Gap before God on Behalf of Others?

The Lord is still looking for those who will stand in the gap on behalf of the land so God will not have to destroy it. Does this challenge grab you? Are you motivated to be that man, or among the men who will commit to standing in the gap before the Lord?

The Ezekiel passage describes one way we can understand the concept of a "gap." In this context, the gap is the huge cleft or chasm between where we are as a people and where we should be with the Lord. This is not merely a moral issue. The Lord does not promote morality apart from relationship with Him. In this sense, the Lord is seeking watchmen who will stand in that gap before the Lord and pray to Him and help lead people back to Him both relationally and morally. In New Testament terms, He is seeking disciples (followers of Jesus) who will make disciples (Matthew 28:18-20).

Men who take the challenge given to us by James the half-brother of Jesus are acting upon God's Word:

> But prove yourselves **doers** of the word, and not just hearers who deceive themselves. For if anyone is a hearer of the word and not a **doer**, he is like a man who looks at his natural face in a mirror; for once he has looked at himself and gone away, he has immediately forgotten what kind of person he was. But one who has looked intently at the perfect law, the law of freedom, and has continued in it, not having become a forgetful hearer but an active **doer**, this person will be blessed in what he **does**. (James 1:22-25 *emphasis added*)

Friends, we don't need more donut-eaters in the church. People who just come on Sunday morning, punch their attendance card, write their checks, have some fellowship with coffee and donuts – then go back home and to work being the same person they were before they went to church. We need "doers" of the Word.

Our salvation is through grace by faith alone in Christ Jesus. Works are evidence of our salvation as we honor God with what we do with the gift(s) he has given us. Sharing our story, passing along biblical truth, loving our neighbors as ourselves, standing up for truth and Kingdom principles, and being available as God directs are some of the action steps an authentic disciple of Christ takes.

Our Sinful Nature

We understand that Jesus Christ is the only one who can ultimately serve as the mediator, the gap filler, between God and mankind. "For there is one God, and one mediator also between God and mankind, the man Christ Jesus, who gave Himself as a ransom for all, the testimony given at the proper time." (1 Timothy 2:5-6) But Jesus calls men and women to follow Him and He sends us out just as the Father sent Him out. Jesus prayed to the Father, "Just as You sent Me into the world, I also sent them into the world" (John 17:18).

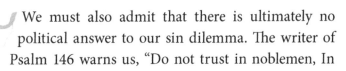 We must also admit that there is ultimately no political answer to our sin dilemma. The writer of Psalm 146 warns us, "Do not trust in noblemen, In

mortal man, in whom there is no salvation. His spirit departs, he returns to the earth; On that very day his plans perish." Instead, "Blessed is he whose help is the God of Jacob, Whose hope is in the Lord his God, ..." (Verses 3-5).

A change in government may help, but it does not address the fallen nature of mankind and our propensity to rebel against God. People need Jesus Christ. Only He can save. Are you willing to be such a man on whom the Lord can count to "stand in the gap before Him on behalf of the people?"

Is There a Gap of Sin in Your Life?

But as followers of Jesus, we must be wary of "gaps" in our own lives as well. One kind of gap is a weakness or vulnerability in our lives. This kind of gap may be a besetting sin, an addiction, an unbridled passion, an idolatrous affection, or a life pattern that we have not yet fully yielded to Christ. If we're honest with ourselves, this sin or pattern has created a rift or gap in our relationship with the Lord. And that gap makes us unproductive in our walk and witness for Christ. We can hardly stand in the gap for others if there are gaping holes in our own life.

I have a friend who is a pastor. He confesses that for many years he would become very angry in traffic only to be smitten in his conscience following such an outburst. He knew this was sinful behavior. His behavior behind the wheel was sometimes rude and obnoxious toward others and dishonoring to God. Each time such an outburst occurred, he repented of his sin asking God to forgive him once again.

As I said, this went on for years, until it all came to a head one day. He had left the church in the afternoon to go hiking before returning to the church to lead a Bible study that night. On his way home a guy cut him off in traffic. At once he angrily blared his horn and gave the guy a dirty look. Once again, the Holy Spirit convicted him of his sinful behavior.

But this time, my friend quailed in remorse. He went on his hike and for the next hour or so, he poured his heart out to God using 1 John 1:9 as his prayer: "If we confess our sins, He is faithful and righteous, so that He will forgive us our sins and cleanse us from all unrighteousness." He prayed through this verse line by line, thought by thought, humbly and in genuine remorse before the Lord.

As he prayed, he expressed that he deeply experienced the Lord's forgiveness and faithfulness. Through Christ, he felt clean again. But during his prayer, the Lord revealed something else to him. My friend recognized that he was living a repeating pattern. He *tried not to get angry* in traffic, but inevitably he did get angry... after which he would repent. It was a cycle he couldn't seem to break.

But then he realized that he had always addressed this anger issue *reactively* instead of *proactively*. He saw for the first time that he needed to go after this sin with the help of the Lord and root it out of his life. It was like a noxious weed in the garden. If all you do is cut it down and the root is still there, it'll come (grow) back. He saw that he needed to expose and pull the root out of his life altogether.

But how? He also recognized that he could not do this on his own strength. Obviously, he needed the Lord's strength, but he also knew that he needed another man in his life, a spiritual mentor to help him root out this sin once and for all.

So, my friend established a relationship with a man whom he trusted and told him about his anger in traffic. He asked him to pray for him, to ride in the car with him, and he gave him permission to ask him how he was doing and to challenge him. My friend also shared this with his wife and asked her to pray with him for deliverance from this sin.

Immediately, my friend began to see a difference in his behavior. To be sure, he had some setbacks, but it has been nearly 20 years since he sought to close that gap in his life and root that sin out, and today he is a different man behind the wheel. Praise God!

What sin, life pattern, idolatrous affection, or evil passion are you wrestling with? What is currently in your life that you feel guilt and shame over? What would you be embarrassed about if your wife, or your pastor, or your children knew? What thing in your life would you like Christ to remove or change?

Go to the Lord in humble confession asking Him not merely to forgive you but to root that thing out of your life that is currently creating a gap in your relationship with Him and others. Go after that sin proactively. Apply Paul's prayer for the Colossians to yourself. He prayed, "… that you will walk in a manner worthy of the Lord, to please Him in all respects, bearing fruit in every good work and increasing in the knowledge of God …" (Colossians 1:10).

Is There a Gap in Your Relationships with Others?

Another thing that causes such a gap in our relationship with the Lord is a rift in our relationships with others. The apostle John explains that it is not possible to love God while hating (or not loving) someone else. It is not possible to love the Father and not love His child. But many of us live with a yawning gap in our relationships with others.

If you know of such a gap or broken relationship in your life, and you're seeking to serve the Lord, "leave your offering there before the altar and go; first be reconciled to your brother, and then come and present your offering" (Matthew 5:24).

This is a tough one. Your intentions could be sincere as you humbly seek reconciliation but the other person in the relationship may not want to reconcile. We have to accept that they may not be in the same place spiritually you are, therefore, they can't participate in bettering the relationship (Rom. 12:18).

Is There a Gap in Your Spiritual Armor?

Yet another kind of gap in our lives may be a gap in our spiritual armor. First Kings, chapter 22 tells the account of King Ahab, the king of Israel, going into battle against the king of Aram. King Ahab knew that he was the trophy that the king of Aram wanted. And indeed, the king of Aram had told his men, "Do not fight with the small or great, but only with the king of Israel" (1 Kings 22:31).

So, King Ahab disguised himself, so that the army of Aram would not recognize him. However, the text explains: "Now one man drew his bow at random and struck the king of Israel in a joint of the armor. ... and he died at evening, ..." (1 Kings 22:34-35).

It does not matter who you are or what your present circumstances are, if you are a follower of Jesus then you are in a spiritual battle. The apostle Peter warns us, "Be of sober spirit, be on the alert. Your adversary, the devil, prowls around like a roaring lion, seeking someone to devour. So resist him, firm in your faith, knowing that the same experiences of suffering are being accomplished by your brothers and sisters who are in the world" (1 Peter 5:8-9).

You and I have a common enemy, the devil. And whether we feel like it or not, we are engaged in battle against him. And just as King Ahab's disguise did not save him, nor will our puny human devices save us from Satan's "arrows." To this end, the Lord has fully equipped us, but we must take full advantage of His equipment, otherwise there will be gaps in our armor.

Some years ago, a friend of mine was hiking in an area one would not consider bear country. But as he started his descent, suddenly he heard a large animal in the dense forest above him rise to its feet. He stopped in his tracks and listened. The animal stopped too and made no further approach. He had seen many moose in the area, so he guessed it was probably a moose.

Not hearing the animal advance, he took a few more steps down the trail, when a black bear rushed down through the foliage and stopped just feet away from him. The bear growled, snarled, and wagged its head menacingly from side-to-side in warning. My friend had no weapon with him but spoke calmly to the bear and slowly backed up the trail until he was out of sight. But since that heart-pounding encounter, my friend always carries bear spray with him!

Unlike that bear, Satan's tactics are usually more subtle, but the danger and impact of his attacks are very real and threatening. The question is not "if" or "whether" Satan will attack, but "when" and "how." We may be able to avoid a bear encounter by not hiking, but there is no earthly remedy for avoiding the attacks of Satan. For this reason, we must be properly prepared and outfitted. The apostle Paul told us how to do this:

Finally, be strong in the Lord and in the strength of His might. Put on the full armor of God, so that you will be able to stand firm against the schemes of the devil. For our struggle is not against flesh and blood, but against the rulers, against the powers, against the world forces of this darkness, against the spiritual forces of wickedness in the heavenly places. Therefore, take up the full armor of God, so that you will be able to resist on the evil day, and having done everything, to stand firm. Stand firm therefore, having belted your waist with truth, and having put on the breastplate of righteousness, and having strapped on your feet the preparation of the gospel of peace; in addition to all, taking up the shield of faith with which you will be able to extinguish all the flaming arrows of the evil one. And take the helmet of salvation and the sword of the Spirit, which is the word of God.

With every prayer and request, pray at all times in the Spirit, and with this in view, be alert with all perseverance and every request for all the saints. (Ephesians 6:10-18)

You and I could not take on a bear attack in our own strength and without a weapon. How much less could we hope to battle Satan in our own strength and without suitable weapons? Paul urges us to "be strong in the Lord and in his mighty power." And to "Put on the full armor of God, so that we can take our stand against the devil's schemes."

I urge you to reread that Scripture above from Ephesians 6 and ask yourself where the gaps are in your armor. Below are some questions to prompt you:

- To what degree are you trying to live the Christian life in your own strength?

- To what extent do you recognize that you're even in a spiritual battle?

- How firm is your stance on the truths of God's Word?

- To what extent are you trusting Christ for forgiveness of sins and right standing with God?

- How ready and willing are you to share the gospel with others?

- What is the integrity of your faith in Christ. Your faith in Christ is your shield, able to extinguish Satan's fiery arrows.

  - Where is your head and mind in terms of your salvation? Are you alert and thinking rightly about your salvation?

- To what extent are you praying with the guidance of the Holy Spirit within you on all occasions?

- How alert are you?

- To what degree are you supporting your fellow "soldiers" in prayer in this supernatural battle?

Perhaps those questions may prompt other questions for you as well. But to aid you in closing any of these gaps in your armor, the next two chapters will focus on two pieces of equipment and how to make the most of them.

Meanwhile, look back over this chapter. Are you willing to stand in the gap before the Lord on behalf of others? What are the gaps of sin in your life that you need to close with the Lord? What are the gaps in your relationships with others? And finally, what are the gaps in your spiritual armor?

Discussion Questions:

To what extent do you desire to be a man who is standing in the gap before the Lord on behalf of others?

What will it take for you to be such a man?

Having read this chapter, what gaps in your life has the Lord revealed to you?

What man do you have in your life who could serve as a spiritual mentor for you? If you do not currently have such a man, how can you go about asking someone to be that spiritual mentor for you?

What other questions do you have after reading this chapter?

Through prayer, God does staggering, miraculous,
overwhelming things. And yet so often by not taking the
time to pray I forget all that deep prayer to God
can accomplish.

CHAPTER 7

Standing in the Gap with God's Word

"I have written to you, young men, because you are strong,
and the word of God remains in you,
and you have overcome the evil one."
– 1 John 2:14 –

When the apostle Paul made his final journey to Jerusalem before being arrested, he stopped in the port of Miletus and sent word to the elders of the church in Ephesus to meet him there. He knew it would be the last time they would see his face, so he spoke to them about things that were most urgent.

In his charge to them Paul warned:

> Be on guard for yourselves and for all the flock,
> among which the Holy Spirit has made you over-
> seers, to shepherd the church of God which He pur-
> chased with His own blood. I know that after my
> departure savage wolves will come in among you,
> not sparing the flock; and from among your own
> selves men will arise, speaking perverse things to
> draw away the disciples after them. Therefore, be
> on the alert, remembering that night and day for a
> period of three years I did not cease to admonish
> each one with tears. (Acts 20:28-31)

Men, Paul's warning doesn't just apply to those elders. Did
you notice that Paul told them that some of these "savage wolves would arise even from their own number"? As
followers of Jesus, we *all* carry the responsibility to "keep
watch," "to be on our guard," and even to watch ourselves.

Paul referred to these troublemakers as "savage wolves"
and Jesus warned us of the same when He said, "Beware of
the false prophets, who come to you in sheep's clothing, but
inwardly are ravenous wolves" (Matthew 7:15).

But how do we keep watch? What does it mean to be on our
guard? How do we recognize false prophets? Jesus

said, "You will know them by their fruits" (Matthew 7:16). But how do we discern between good and bad "fruit"?

The answer to those questions is largely by knowing God's Word intimately and letting it permeate our lives. God's Word is the standard. His Word is the filter through which we discern whether someone is genuine or a wolf in sheep's clothing. And as Jesus explained, it's not merely a matter of having the right theology or right doctrinal statement. It's also a matter of the "fruit" of a person's life as guided by the Scriptures.

As a friend of mine likes to put it, "It's easy to clean the outside of the cup, but it's the inside of the cup that needs to be cleaned by the Word of God and by His Spirit."

The need for godly watchmen who will stand in the gap on behalf of their families, their churches, and their nation is as pressing today as it has ever been.

In previous chapters, we talked about how the Lord challenges us men to stand in the gap before Him on behalf of others. Given the current state of our country, the need for men to stand in the gap before the Lord on behalf of our families and country is as great as ever before.

We also urged each of us to consider whether there are gaps of sin in our lives, gaps in our relationships with others, or gaps in our spiritual armor. Attention to God's Word is essential in addressing any of these gaps in our lives. And need I say, you and I do NOT want to be one of those "men even from your own number who will arise and distort the truth in order to draw away disciples after them." We must keep watch over our own hearts!

Even when writing to his mentee Timothy, the apostle Paul warned him, "Pay close attention to yourself and to the teaching; …" (1 Timothy 4:16). The same applies to us.

God's Word reveals, "for all have sinned and fall short of the glory of God" (Romans 3:23). "All have sinned." No one is exempt. We all fall short… we all miss the mark of God's glory… of God's holiness.

And how would we know where or how we fall short of God's holiness apart from His revealed Word? How would we know what is pleasing to Him and what dishonors and offends Him apart from knowing Him? And how can we know Him unless we get to know Him through His revealed Word?

Mankind left to himself, and his own devices is in constant rebellion against God. Look around at the signs of our fallen condition. In our own ignorance and perverted wisdom, we not only call what is evil good, but we promote it and celebrate it. Left to ourselves, we've lost all sense of right and wrong. This leaves huge gaps in our relationship with God and others, gaps in what's morally right, and gaps in simply conducting our lives.

 Think of God's Word in terms of home construction or woodworking. Without a blueprint, a square, a tape measure, and a level, how could we build a home? We'd only be guessing at how straight and true our construction is. Building a home without those tools, we would have no standard. There would be no soundness in its construction. There's no way it could pass inspection.

Or think of God's Word in terms of a service manual for an automobile. Unless we know what, the manufacturer calls for in the numerous adjustments and settings required to keep the engine running well, we're only guessing at what's required. And left to our own estimates, we may ruin the engine altogether. We need the service manual.

Or imagine a SWAT team surrounding a terrorist hideout, bursting through the front and back doors to confront these armed terrorists... but they do so without any weapons! Attempting to overrun a terrorist cell without weapons would be foolhardy and deadly!

Or think of God's Word as a light. What if you were exploring the depths of an uncharted cave with all its twists and turns and squeeze-through passageways? You're a mile into the cavern and suddenly your source of light goes out! You're left in utter darkness and attempting to feel your way out is impossible.

On the heel of all those examples, you might be thinking, "Alright, already! I get it! I need God's Word in my life!"

How can we think we can build our lives, or a society without the necessary tools, or a proper guide?

How can we hope to find our way out of the oppressive darkness of a cavern without a light? How can we think we could defend ourselves or our loved ones without adequate weapons? In the same way, we desperately need God's Word!

But our need for God's Word goes even more deeply than that. Consider what the Lord meant when He declared, "Man does not live on bread alone but on every word that comes from the mouth of the Lord" (Matthew 4:4; Deuteronomy 8:3). God's Word is the very sustenance of life. Jeremiah declared, "When I discovered your words, I devoured them. They are my joy and my heart's delight, for I bear your name, O Lord God of Heaven's Armies" (Jeremiah 15:16 NLT).

Think about the following Scriptures:[9]

- Psalm 33:4, "For the word of the Lord is right, And all His work is done in faithfulness."

- Psalm 119:9, 11, "How can a young man keep his way pure? By keeping it according to Your word. I have treasured Your word in my heart, So that I may not sin against You."

- Psalm 119:105, "Your word is a lamp to my feet And a light to my path."

---

9   These Scriptures taken from the New American Standard Bible. (NASB)

- Hebrews 4:12, "For the word of God is living and active, and sharper than any two-edged sword, even penetrating as far as the division of soul and spirit, of both joints and marrow, and able to judge the thoughts and intentions of the heart."

- Ephesians 6:17, "And take … the sword of the Spirit, which is the word of God."

But a sword is of little use to a soldier unless he knows how to wield it.

I have a friend who served in the Army during the Viet Nam War. He explains that in Basic Training, recruits were drilled on the proper maintenance and use of the M-16 assault rifle. They became so familiar with the weapon that all their actions with it became reflexive. In a combat situation, you don't have time to think about or grapple with how to clear a jammed round. That response must become second nature, automatic and instantaneous.

Standing in the Gap

One of my favorite books of the Bible is Nehemiah. For 70 years the Israelites had been held captive in a foreign land due to their repeated rebellion against God. Finally, they were permitted to return to their homeland and rebuild Jerusalem. But the walls of that great city were in rubble and there were huge gaps through which their enemies could attack. God called Nehemiah to return to Jerusalem and provide leadership for rebuilding the wall.

Their enemies constantly harassed and harangued the Jews trying to build. So, Nehemiah stationed armed guards next to the workers and many workers worked with a tool in one hand and a sword in the other. But with these precautions and under Nehemiah's leadership, they rebuilt the wall in just 52 days. In this way they completely frustrated the efforts of their enemies.

The spiritual battle we face today is no less real. But the gaps we face today are of a different kind. In the schools, our children are being brainwashed into believing they can choose their gender. White children are told they are the problem and responsible for all the social ills of our nation, while children of color hear that they are poor victims.

Meanwhile our culture is legitimizing, promoting, and celebrating homosexuality, the transgender lifestyle, same-sex marriage, child porn, and a myriad of other aberrant sexual activities. Some sources indicate that more than half of all American men engage in pornography, which is the exploitation of women.

Lying, deception, censorship, blackmail, and all sorts of other nefarious activities are commonplace even among our country's leaders. I could go on and on, but I'll let you fill in the blanks. We are in far worse straights than Jerusalem in Nehemiah's day. The gaps are in our homes, in our schools, in our places of work, and in our lives.

Attention to God's Word was paramount to Nehemiah's success in rebuilding the wall and closing the gaps—not only in the physical wall—but in the moral and spiritual lives of Jerusalem's inhabitants as well. For this purpose, Nehemiah worked with Ezra the priest. They gathered all the inhabitants of Jerusalem: men, women, and children to hear the Word of God.

From daybreak until noon, Ezra read from the Book of the Law (God's Word). Then, many of the Levites continued to read God's Word and instruct the people, "They read from the book, from the Law of God, translating to give the sense so that they understood the reading" (Nehemiah 8:8).

Initially, those who listened to God's Word were cut to the heart over their sin and rebellion and they confessed their sins and repented. Then, having done so, they rejoiced in God's goodness. The Scripture says, "Then all the people went away to eat, drink, to send portions, and to celebrate a great feast, because they understood the words which had been made known to them" (Nehemiah 8:12). And in the days to follow, they continued in God's Word.

We've taken a brief look at some of the gaps in our lives. So, what does it look like to stand in the gap with God's Word? How do we become adept at applying it in all the situations that life throws at us? When the Bible says that God's Word is the sword of the Spirit, we can make the mistake of thinking that all we need to do is known a few key verses and start slashing! But Paul challenges us, "Be diligent to present yourself approved to God as a worker who does not need to be ashamed, accurately handling the word of truth" (2 Timothy 2:15).

The Lord uses many different metaphors in the Bible to describe the various characteristics of His Word. He speaks of His Word as a *sword* in Ephesians 6:17 and Hebrews 4:12; as a *lamp* in Psalm 119:105; as *seed* in Luke 8:11; as *food* in Deuteronomy 8:3 and Jeremiah 15:16; *more precious than gold* in Psalm 19:10; and in many other ways.

Through God's Word we gain wisdom and understanding, and we receive "instruction in wise behavior" and prudence (Proverbs 1:2, 4). Through God's Word we can understand what it means to fear the Lord, and "... discern righteousness, justice, wnd integrity, and every good path" (Proverbs 2:5, 9).

But again, how do we do this? How do we "correctly handle the word of truth as approved workers of God"?

Men, we are generally goal-oriented. This goal orientation and our ability to discipline ourselves can either work for us or against us. For instance, one man might say, "Okay, I'll commit to reading three chapters in the Bible every day." And perhaps he sticks with it until he has read through the whole Bible. Then what? And what was his frame of mind and heart as he read the Bible?

Do we have to attend an intense weekly Bible study, or even attend Bible college or seminary? Is that what it takes to thoroughly know God's Word?

All those ideas might serve to help us "correctly handle the word of truth," but they also may not help us and here's why. My friend Rob shares his experience:

> I came to Christ as a child and I started reading the Bible every day from the age of 11, because someone told me that's what good Christians do. But after a while, I realized I was just going through the motions. I mistakenly saw reading the Bible as a work, a way to stay in God's good graces. "A chapter a day keeps the devil away," or something like that.
>
> There was also a lot in the Bible that I didn't understand. So, day after day I read without getting much out of it. I confess that I was often distracted and even bored while reading the Bible.
>
> After high school, I attended Bible college for a semester before running out of funds. I look back on my experience in Bible college at that time and must admit that I was there simply to have a good time and hung around with the wrong crowd. I didn't apply myself in my studies, so my grades were poor, and I got little out of it. My priorities were all wrong and I neglected my relationship with the Lord.
>
> I left college and got a job in a feed mill in Minneapolis, MN to pay off my school debt. In

that rough, secular work environment, I met two young men who had recently come to Christ out of the hippie culture. Their love for God and others was contagious and apparent to all. On every break they would pull a tattered New Testament out of their pockets and devour God's Word.

After watching those two guys for a couple weeks and witnessing the dynamic nature of their relationship with God, I went home one evening and dropped to my knees next to my bed. I begged God to give me the kind of relationship with Him that I saw modeled by those two men. And my life has not been the same since!

One of the notable changes that occurred in my life was my approach to God's Word. Instead of mindlessly reading the Bible as a discipline, I now hunger to know God better. I go to God's Word to meet with Him. I want to hear His voice in His Word and commune with Him. I want to learn what pleases Him and obey Him. I want to pattern my life according to His Word.

Reading, studying, and memorizing God's Word is like eating to me. Nobody has to force me to eat! I look forward to a meal thinking about what I'll eat, how good it'll taste, and who I'll enjoy it with. Also, as long as we're alive, we'll never arrive at a place where we no longer have to eat. The same is true for us with God's Word.

As I read through Rob's testimony, the thing that strikes me is his approach to God's Word—that he always goes to the Word with the intent to meet with God. This relational approach to God's Word is something that I practice as well, and it changes everything.

You see, when we read the Bible expecting to meet with God, we get to know Him personally and we find ourselves on a trajectory of life change in Him. As we draw near to Him and get to know Him better, He changes us. In fact, it's impossible to draw near to God and remain unchanged.

This is what Jesus meant when He talked about abiding or remaining or living in Him. In John 15:5 He said, "I am the vine, you are the branches; the one who remains in Me, and I in him bears much fruit, for apart from Me you can do nothing." Then, a couple verses later He equates remaining in Him with remaining in His words and His words remaining in us.

This is what it means to stand in the gap with God's Word. As we abide in Christ and His Word, He closes those gaps of sin in our lives, gaps in our relationships, gaps in our spiritual armor, and gaps in the dangers lurking in our culture. When we remain in Christ, we bear much fruit, but apart from Him we can do nothing.

The apostle James wrote, "But prove yourselves doers of the word, and not just hearers who deceive themselves" (James 1:22). Merely listening to or reading the word mindlessly deceives us into thinking that we're doing something good, or that this mindless activity is somehow magically helping us. James calls this deception.

If you don't currently read the Bible regularly, I urge you to do so. But get into the Word to spend time with your Lord. Always go to the Word with the intent to meet with God. Get to know Him better and learn how to abide in (or remain in or live in) Him. Put His Word into action in your life.

> Blessed is the person who does not walk in the
> counsel of the wicked,
> Nor stand in the path of sinners,
> Nor sit in the seat of scoffers!
> But his delight is in the Law of the Lord,
> And on His Law he meditates day and night.
> He will be like a tree planted by streams of water,
> Which yields its fruit in its season,
> And its leaf does not wither;
> And in whatever he does, he prospers.
> (Psalm 1:1-3)

When we actively apply the Word of God in our lives, the Lord uses us and His Word within us to fill the gaps in our family, at work, in our community, and beyond.

May we cry out with the Psalmist, "Oh, how I love your Word! I meditate on it all day long" (Psalm 119:97 *paraphrased*).

But you may wonder, "How do I keep this attitude and approach to God's Word alive and vibrant? How do I prevent myself from just going through the motions, or even failing to stay in the Word?"

I know of no better way than by meeting regularly with a spiritual mentor. A spiritual mentor is someone with whom you can be honest and real. "As iron sharpens iron, so one man sharpens another" (Proverbs 27:17 *paraphrased*).

When you meet with your spiritual mentor, share what the Lord is doing in your lives. Discuss Scripture passages that you're currently reading or studying and pray with and for each other. I'll share more about spiritual mentorship in another chapter.

Discussion Questions:

What is your current practice in terms of reading and studying God's Word?

How has the Lord spoken to your recently through His Word?

Discuss the statement: "Always go to the Word with the intent to meet with God."

What will you change or initiate as a result of reading this chapter?

"One thing, and only one thing, is necessary for the Christian life, righteousness, and freedom. That one thing is the most holy Word of God, the gospel of Christ."

– Martin Luther

CHAPTER 8

Standing in the Gap through Prayer

"Keep watching and praying, so that you do not come into temptation; the spirit is willing, but the flesh is weak."

– Matthew 26:41 –

As I write this, we have just passed another anniversary of the attack on Pearl Harbor on December 7, 1941. On that day, 2,403 Americans were killed, four US battleships were sunk and others damaged, and 188 aircraft were destroyed and many others damaged. One of the greatest factors that led to our surprise over the attack was a failure to get an urgent *communication* to Pearl Harbor that an attack might be imminent.

One of the most strategic elements of any war or battle is communication. Take the enemy's communication lines down, and they lose the ability to coordinate and mobilize his army. Prayer is our communication line with the Lord.

Consider another infamous day that we previously mentioned in another chapter. It is worth revisiting for this illustration. The night on which our Lord was arrested in the Garden of Gethsemane, what were the disciples doing? Jesus knew very well what was about to happen, but His disciples were clueless despite His attempts to warn them.

So, on the night Jesus and His disciples retreated to Gethsemane, Jesus said to them, "My soul is deeply grieved, to the point of death; remain here and keep watch with Me" (Matthew 26:38). But as Jesus prayed fervently, His disciples did not watch but kept falling asleep. Three times Jesus got up and went back to His disciples saying, "So, you men could not keep watch with Me for one hour? Keep watching and praying, so that you do not come into temptation; the spirit is willing, but the flesh is weak" (Verses 40-41).

The Lord repeatedly warns us: "Watch out that no one deceives you;" and "Therefore be on the alert, for you do not know which day your Lord is coming" (Matthew 24:4, 42). And in the passage on spiritual armor, Paul exhorts us to "… pray at all times in the Spirit, and with this in view, be alert with all perseverance and every request for all the saints" (Ephesians 6:18). The concept of watchfulness is strategically tied with prayer in Scripture.

What is Prayer?

Prayer is a special communication system with God Almighty. Through prayer we can go to God and share our dreams, concerns, fears, ambitions, requests, and praise (Philippians 4:6). As a foghorn helps direct a lost fisherman or sailor back to port, so an active prayer life gives guidance and vision to help us through the fog of life. So important was prayer to Christ that He often withdrew from the crowds for the sole purpose of praying (Luke 5:16).

In his book, *How to Pray*, E. Stanley Jones tells us that "Prayer is not only the refuge of the weak; it is the reinforcement of the strong." Jones goes on to suggest that "Prayer is not bending God to my will, but it is a bringing of my will into conformity with God's will, so that His will may work in and through me. Prayer is not bending the universe to your will, making God a cosmic bellhop for your purposes, but prayer is cooperating with the purposes of God to do things you never dreamed you could do."[10]

During Jesus' ministry, He was praying one time and "when He finished, one of His disciples said to Him, 'Lord, teach us to pray'" (Luke 11:1). Jesus responded by giving them an example of how they might pray, a prayer we call "The Lord's Prayer." Here is that prayer as recorded by Matthew:

---

10   E. Stanley Jones, *How to Pray* (Nashville, TN: Abingdon Press, 1979), p.5&6.

Pray, then, in this way:
'Our Father, who is in heaven,
Hallowed be Your name.
Your kingdom come.
Your will be done, On earth as it is in heaven.
Give us this day our daily bread.
And forgive us our debts, as we also have forgiven
our debtors.
And do not lead us into temptation,
but deliver us from evil."
(Matthew 6:9-13)

Notice how *short* this prayer is. And it is directed to *"our Father* in heaven." This is very personal. You are His child, and He is your Father. This short prayer contains elements of praise, worship, dependence, requests, confession, submission to His will, and intent to obey.

I am convinced that prayer is so simple, even a child can pray effectively. But our enemy, the evil one, has so confused men about prayer that many men complicate it or feel totally inept at praying. Being transparent, I confess to you that I too struggled with prayer as a young man. If you are also among us who have struggled with prayer, you're in good company!

When Jesus gave His disciples (and us) this prayer, He literally said, "Pray like this," and not "pray these words." Of course, it's totally okay to pray The Lord's

Prayer, but ultimately Jesus gave this prayer as a *model* or *example* of *how to pray*. God's Word is full of other great prayers that we can pray or borrow from and integrate into our own prayers. Many of the Psalms are prayers. Consider the following examples:[11]

"Lord, our Lord, how majestic is your name in all the earth." (Psalm 8:1)

"You will make known to me the way of life; In Your presence is fullness of joy; In Your right hand there are pleasures forever." (Psalm 16:11)

"I have called upon You, for You will answer me, God; Incline Your ear to me, hear my speech." (Psalm 17:6)

"Also keep Your servant back from presumptuous sins; Let them not rule over me; Then I will be innocent, And I will be blameless of great wrongdoing. May the words of my mouth and the meditation of my heart Be acceptable in Your sight, Lord, my rock and my Redeemer." (Psalm 19:12-14)

"How great is Your goodness, Which You have stored up for those who fear You, Which You have performed for those who take refuge in You, Before the sons of mankind!" (Psalm 31:19)

---

11   All of these passages are from the NIV.

"Whom do I have in heaven but You? And with You, I desire nothing on earth." (Psalm 73:25)

How to Pray

I think you get the idea. At the same time, it's not necessary to integrate prayers from the Bible into our prayers, we can also simply speak to the Lord from our hearts.

As I mentioned above, the Lord's Prayer offers us a model of some of the content that we might pray. Someone has also suggested the acrostic ACTS as a way to remember what content we might include in our prayers. That acrostic works out to **A**=Adoration, **C**=Confession, **T**=Thanksgiving, and S=Supplication or requests. And while knowing the ACTS acrostic may be helpful, there is so much more to praying.

For instance, I would venture to say that most of us consider prayer a one-way conversation. We talk, God listens. But a monologue is a poor method of communication. What if we were to communicate with our wives like that?

What if we told our spouses: "Honey, I'm going to talk to you for twenty minutes each morning—all you have to do is listen. Then, at mealtimes and before bed, I'll speak to you briefly again, without any talking on your part."

I know that my wife would tell me I could take my communication plan and stuff it! That's not communing and communicating with each other. That's simply reciting a monologue or speech.

Personally, it took me many years to recognize that in prayer I needed to be quiet and let the Lord speak to me too. I'm not trying to get weird on you here. I've never heard God's voice audibly during my prayer times. But the Lord urges us, "Stop striving and know that I am God; I will be exalted among the nations, I will be exalted on the earth" (Psalm 46:10). And the Scriptures clearly tell us that God reveals things to us by His Spirit (1 Corinthians 2:10).

In addition to hearing good messages, seeking wise counsel, searching for the "open doors and pathways" that tell me I'm heading the right direction, listening to my wife, and meditating on God's Word – prayer is how God reveals Himself to me. His Spirit shapes my image of how to approach problems, find relief from anxiety, quicken my heart to important decisions, and convict me of my sinfulness.

A senior pastor friend of mine was asked by the associate pastor how he could become better at praying. The senior pastor made a unique recommendation. Living in Southern California, the desert was a short drive from the church. He told the associate pastor to drive out into the desert, make a camp, bring enough food and water for three days, and pray. He could only bring his Bible in his belongings – no other books or magazines and certainly not electronic gadgets or communication devices. He couldn't even listen to the radio in his car.

But when he began praying, within a few minutes he was done and at a loss what to do with the rest with the rest of his three days! Initially having two

103

days to pray seemed like an impossibility then the young pastor began to feel the hand of God upon his life and thought process.

So, this young man went back to his pastor and explained the transformation that happened in his prayer life. His pastor gave him the following assignment. He told him to set aside 20 minutes each day for 30 days for prayer. He instructed him to go somewhere he could be alone and simply to sit quietly before the Lord and listen as much as he prayed. This is how God can speak to our hearts.

This young man followed through with this advice. For the first week, he confesses that his mind would wander, and he had to continually bring himself back to a consciousness of the Lord's presence. But after a week or so, he began to "hear" promptings from the Lord about people to pray for and things that he needed to change in his own life. He was beginning to experience a two-way conversation with the Lord. And because the Holy Spirit lives in us, why should we think this unusual?

My experience in growing in prayer has been similar. Nowadays, in the morning, I get up early and grab a little breakfast and hot beverage and head to my quiet office. Once my dog gets his biscuit, he leaves the room, and my quiet time begins. I read God's Word and speak to Him too, thanking Him, praising Him, and sometimes pouring my heart out to Him. Sometimes I bounce ideas off Him, asking for His leadership. I confess my sins and ask Him to make me more like Him. And I share my requests with Him, which are mostly about the needs of others. But the general tenor of my prayer time with the Lord is one in which I enjoy His presence and His fellowship as I sit quietly before Him and listen. Then, throughout the day, at any time and in any place, I'll talk to Him some more and ask Him to speak to me.

The Lord is the one Person we can be totally honest and transparent with, because He already knows everything about us anyway. You might ask, "If God already knows everything about me, why do I have to tell Him what He already knows?"

First, this isn't a matter of our *having to tell* Him, rather it's a matter of *wanting to* because He's our Heavenly Father.

Second, when our kids were teenagers, we encouraged them to come to us anytime with anything. No matter what it was, we wanted to hear from them. We wanted them to know that we were always available to them. So, when one of our boys would knock on our door at 10:30pm and throw himself at the foot of our bed and pour his heart out to us, we wouldn't turn him away, but listen to the longings and trials of his young life.

We need to see our Father in Heaven as that kind of parent, so that we too will readily come to Him with anything and everything, knowing that He takes greater interest in our daily pursuits than we can possibly imagine. Let me be even more specific: He cares about everything we say and do. Nothing we bring to Him is too trivial for Him to care about.

So, what does prayer have to do with being watchful and standing in the gap for our family, our friends, and our nation?

At the beginning of the book of Nehemiah, when he heard that those who had survived the exile in Jerusalem were in great trouble and disgrace and that Jerusalem's walls were broken down and its gates burned, the first thing Nehemiah did was pray. Nehemiah recorded, "Now when I heard these words, I sat down and wept and mourned for days; and I was fasting and praying before the God of heaven" (Nehemiah 1:4). Then, he wrote down the gist of his prayers to the Lord.

What is so important to see from Nehemiah's conversation with the Lord is that through that prayer, the Lord moved Nehemiah to be His man who would go to Jerusalem to repair the wall and its gates, and to help the Israelites in their troubles and disgrace. Prayer sets everything in motion. Nehemiah's prayer is what God used to get him to Jerusalem.

Then, when Nehemiah was overseeing the rebuilding of the walls of Jerusalem, he established a communication system among the workers. Back then, it was a horn blast. When the enemy would attack a particular gap in the wall, the watchmen guarding there would blow the ram's horn to call for reinforcements to close that gap and prevent the enemy from intruding.

While Nehemiah oversaw the rebuilding of the walls, he experienced repeated attempts by their enemies to oppose the work. In those times, he constantly turned to the Lord in prayer for strength, wisdom, and resolve. Remarkably, and to the disgrace of their enemies, they rebuilt the walls in just 52 days!

As we continue reading Nehemiah, prayer played such a prominent role, not only in rebuilding the walls of Jerusalem, but in rebuilding the people's trust and dependence upon the Lord, for they had been beaten down. Through Nehemiah, the people in Jerusalem experienced a revival in their love for the Lord and in righteous living. In Nehemiah, we see how one man's watchfulness and willingness to stand in the gap for his people changed the course of history, and it all began and continued with prayer.

How about you? You may think, "I'm no Nehemiah!" But God has placed you where you are in all your relationships with your family, your church, your work, your community, and this nation. Will you purpose to be a watchman for the Lord on behalf of those within the scope of your relationships? Begin in prayer and learn to sit quietly in God's presence and hear His voice.

Discussion Questions:

Describe your experience with prayer so far in your walk with the Lord.

What are your biggest challenges when it comes to prayer?

Discuss what it means to sit quietly before the Lord and listen to Him.

What other questions do you have about prayer?

Based on this chapter and your discussion, what will you commit to regarding standing in the gap for others through prayer?

It doesn't matter what is in front of you if you can trust the support of the men behind you.

CHAPTER 9

Standing in the Gap with Other Men

"Bear one another's burdens, and so fulfill the law of Christ."
– Galatians 6:2 ESV –

I've had the privilege of doing several ride-alongs with various police and fire departments as I fulfilled my role as chaplain for first responders. You definitely see a different side of life when you hang out with these guys. It is common for first responders to share their "tales of woe or war stories" after a close encounter with those who will listen. Actually, it is officially called a "debrief" on major incidents.

Hearing these exchanges is like listening to a group of fishermen or hunters who take delight in expressing the challenges and victories of their outdoor adventures. The very nature of being a chaplain doesn't allow me to share many of the experiences I've encountered without breaking confidence, but there was one adventure that bears repeating as it relates to the title of this chapter.

It was my custom to ride with the duty officer or command sergeant as he or she responded to the most important incidents. One Friday evening a huge hard-rock concert was taking place at a large venue in Post Falls, Idaho where we live. That night we were down two officers beside the sergeant due to illness and a scheduling problem; hence, coverage was very limited.

Our car and another officer's car were the only units near the venue. The concert was coming to an end when a large fight broke out between some Native Americans and a few Rednecks. Fists were flying, blood was spilling, and people were yelling.

Our car arrived on scene just as the concert goers were leaving. The roads were totally plugged with outgoing traffic; therefore, no other support vehicle could cover us. We were on our own.

The sergeant pulled up to the fight and jumped out of his unit. I could see that he wouldn't be able to anticipate anyone coming up behind him or handle the size of the group beginning to surround him. Despite all his tactical gear and professional experience, standing alone was not going to be enough.

Instinctively, I jumped out of the vehicle with no weapons in my possession. I felt in the darkness that the police uniform and badge I was wearing might be enough to let people know my sergeant wasn't alone in this confrontation. It brought back memories of the days I lived in East Oakland when fighting was part of my existence during my younger years.

We were able to separate the fighting parties and get them out of the venue without any more struggles. After about a half-hour we sat back in the vehicle, both of us taking a deep breath realizing this could have really gone in a different direction.

The Sergeant glared at me and said, "You aren't supposed to get out of the vehicle in this type of situation, but I'm sure glad you did. Your presence made a statement that I wasn't alone against this whole crowd. Thank you Chap! You had my six."

I responded to the sergeant that my reactions were from Scripture. No man should have to stand alone. The Sergeant was young in his faith but identified with the following thoughts from God's Word that I shared with him:

> "For where two or three have gathered together in My name, I am there in their midst." (Matthew 18:20)

"And if one can overpower him who is alone, two can resist him. A cord of three strands is not quickly torn apart." (Ecclesiastes 4:12)

Do you know someone who is trying to stand alone? Can you think of a time you've been there for someone who is engaged in a battle that needs someone watching his six?

Who is Watching Your Six?

Best-selling author Dave Ramsey shares an observation that helps us define terms and capture the reality of the moment.

You remember Snoopy and the Red Baron? They flew what's called a biplane with a machine gun mounted in front of the pilot. In World War I, pilots flew biplanes for the first time and the battle was taken to the air. To shoot down an enemy plane, the pilot had to line up above or in front to shoot directly into the other plane and kill the enemy pilot or at least his engine. But the safest and most efficient position for the shot was to fly in behind the enemy, allowing continuous fire and a more likely strike.

In the military, they use a clock to inform positions. Twelve o'clock is straight above you. Six o'clock is straight behind you and sets up the best strike zone. WWI pilots were the first to say, "I got your six," meaning they've got you covered so the enemy can't come up behind your back and kill you.

"I got your six" means "I got your back." It declares a story of loyalty . . . *I'm loyal to you. I've got you covered. You're safe from enemies stabbing you in the back if I'm around.*[12]

One of the features inherent with men's small groups is developing loyalty and trust. Taking on the responsibility of checking in with someone who is struggling or going through a difficult challenge. The expressions "I've got your six" means a great deal to most men who are struggling to find their way through difficulties. According to Barna Research it is estimated that over 70% of men do not have a trusted confidant, a man at their six, who they can count on to be there when there is a crisis.

I think we should all learn how to be a confidant for the people and the organizations we care about. We should develop the character qualities of loyalty, grace, and forgiveness to assure others that they can trust us. We shouldn't stab people in the back. We should earn people's trust by being trustworthy. We should be known for standing in the gap for brothers and applying God's Word to the situation. After all, He is our rock:

---

12   https://www.ramseysolutions.com/personal-growth/i-got-your-six.

Then the Lord said, "Behold, there is a place by Me, and you shall stand there on the rock." (Exodus 33:21)

"... and all drank the same spiritual drink, for they were drinking from a spiritual rock which followed them; and the rock was Christ." (1 Corinthians 10:4)

"Therefore, take up the full armor of God, so that you will be able to resist on the evil day, and having done everything, to stand firm. Stand firm therefore, having belted your waist with truth, and having put on the breastplate of righteousness, and having strapped on your feet the preparation of the gospel of peace." (Ephesians 6:13-15)

"Fear not, for I am with you. Do not be dismayed. I am your God. I will strengthen you; I will help you; I will uphold you with my victorious right hand." (Joshua 1:9 ESV)

God's Watchman and Warriors

Earlier in this book I provided a definition of Watchman: A "Kingdom Man" or "Kingdom Warrior" (in referencing Authentic Manhood) is equivalent to a Watchman. A person who stands in the gap for others. Have you ever met a real warrior? Maybe someone who has gone to battle, a first responder, a person protecting their family, or maybe a pastor willing to take a stand against the Woke environment we live in?

A trusted warrior isn't the ridiculous Hollywood version of the steroid-laced macho-man. I'm talking about a true warrior; someone who will have your back when needed and who stands strong during personal attacks. They are a different breed. Warriors carry themselves differently than most people. They speak with purpose and boldly proclaim and mimic the life of Christ in their daily living.

They are not people who usually stand out in the crowd. However, others will look to them in times of great difficulty. You won't hear a true warrior bragging about how awesome they are or about the things they have done. Most warriors have a great degree of humility. A warrior may have a sense of humor, but he never plays the fool. Warriors usually have a quiet confidence that comes from another source. When you meet a true warrior, you will know it. Simply put, warriors operate differently than most people.

If Christians embraced the ethic and discipline of warriors who take the "six" for their bothers, our world would see radical change in love, leadership, and sacrifice.

I like how author Dace Clifton puts it:

Being a Christian and a warrior are two ideas seldom connected in the modern world. Many people associate Christianity more with weakness than strength. Some prefer to think of Christians as soft, pliable, and accommodating. Others have far worse opinions of Christians. Sadly, I can think of more than one example that reinforces a bad stereotype. However, I'm convinced Christians should be warriors. Let me explain. I'll start with a qualification: I'm not remotely suggesting that Christian ideals or spiritual change should be enacted through physical violence, making bombs, or any other crazy and unbiblical idea. I am referring to the embrace of a warrior's ethic and mindset. If Christians embraced the ethic and discipline of warriors, our world would see radical change. I believe this shift would cause an unparalleled resurgence of strength, leadership, sacrifice, courage, and love in our world. Below are a few observations on embracing a warrior's ethic as a Christian.

A warrior is humbly seeking God's will in his life. He looks for opportunities to serve and defend the rights and freedom of others. He gives God the credit and glorifies Him with his work, diligence, and character.

One of the things that separates warriors from others is the price they are willing to pay. Warriors train long hours. They endure great difficulties and pain. They are willing to sacrifice their own personal comfort, preferences, and selfish desires. Every sacrifice is made in the service of a greater cause. Few people become warriors because they are unwilling to pay the real price. Most people are unwilling to make significant and long-term sacrifices. The price is high to be a true warrior. Plus, the costs are ongoing. Sacrifice goes well beyond some initial period of training. Warriors sacrifice a lifestyle.

Great sacrifice is required to be a Christian. Jesus spoke clearly about what it takes to follow him. Luke 9:23 says: "And He was saying to them all, 'If anyone wants to come after Me, he must deny himself, take up his cross daily, and follow Me'" Being a Christian is awesome. The price for my sin is paid in full by Christ. I cannot earn salvation, nor am I paying it out on an installment plan. With that said, we must recognize that following Jesus is costly business. Sacrifice will be required. A person cannot follow Jesus and remain where they are… they are going to have to move forward. Movement involves sacrifice. Don't kid yourself: following Jesus is wonderful, but very costly. Following Jesus is a radical lifestyle change. If you see no change, you are not following Jesus. A Christianity without sacrifice is not the faith I read about in the Bible. It costs you something to be a Christian. Jesus tells us to count the cost before we make this all-important decision (see Luke 14:27-33).[13]

---

13   http://dailypastor.com Dace Clifton Being a Warrior for God, Part Two.

Warriors and Watchman Are Encouragers to Others

One of the most important traits of a successful warrior or watchman is being humble as he helps others in their journey. God's Word provides a roadmap of direction for us to follow. Those of us standing in the gap for others should remind ourselves about these admonitions regularly.

"My brothers, if anyone among you wanders from the truth and someone brings him back, let him know that whoever brings back a sinner from his wandering will save his soul from death and will cover a multitude of sins." (James 5:19-20 ESV)

"Not neglecting to meet together, as is the habit of some, but encouraging one another, and all the more as you see the Day drawing near." (Hebrews 10:25 ESV)

"Let the word of Christ dwell in you richly, teaching and admonishing one another in all wisdom, singing psalms and hymns and spiritual songs, with thankfulness in your hearts to God." (Colossians 3:16 ESV)

"Take care, brothers, lest there be in any of you an evil, unbelieving heart, leading you to fall away from the living God. But exhort one another every day, as long as it is called "today," that none

of you may be hardened by the deceitfulness of sin."
(Hebrews 3:12-13 ESV)

Standing in the Gap Means We Are Encouragers

When we look at lives of Nehemiah and Ezekiel, we see men who knew how to motivate others. They were men who found ways to inspire and encourage others to take on tasks greater than they could have imagined. A person who is successful in standing in the gap for other men is ultimately a great encourager. He finds ways to challenge others to be stronger and more apt to tackle difficult tasks.

Encouraging someone is a simple thing yet often neglected in our self-centered culture. The "me generation" seems to place more emphasis on individualism than on teamwork. As Christians we are instructed to be encouragers. Larry Crab Jr. and Dan Allender in their outstanding work on encouragement wrote:

> Christians are commanded to encourage one another. Because words have the power to affect people deeply, it is appropriate to consider how to encourage fellow Christians through what we say. Words can encourage, discourage, or do nothing. We must learn to speak sincerely with positive impact, using

our works to help other Christians pursue the pathway of obedience more zealously.[14]

The act of inspiring others should be fundamental to our faith. There are many lessons on encouragement in Scripture but none more powerful than two from our Savior's life.

How important is this topic? Even God chose to publicly commend, inspire, and encourage Jesus. As an assembled crowd looked on, John the Baptist blessed and baptized Jesus in the Jordan River. God appreciated the moment and the willingness of Christ to apply himself to the call. God the Father proclaimed, "This is My beloved Son, in whom I am well pleased" (Matthew 3:17 ESV). And again the same supporting message was proclaimed at the end of His ministry as recorded by Matthew: "This is my Son, with whom I am well pleased; listen to Him" (Matthew 17:5 ESV)! Did the God-man, Jesus, really need to be encouraged? Probably not, but by way of modeling this principal God provided words of encouragement so we could see how important it is to our purpose and success.

What was God saying? It appears that these chosen words were intended to convey His support, approval, love, and acceptance. Wasn't He really saying, "I LOVE YOU, I'M PROUD OF YOU!"?

14   Lawrence J. Crabb, Jr. and Dan B. Allender, *Encouragement*, (Grand Rapids, MI: Zondervan Publishing House, 1984), p.25.

Encouragement – a simple thing yet often neglected. As Christians we are instructed to be encouragers.

Encouragement—A Powerful Motivator

We often forget that encouraging others is one of the most powerful motivators available to us. There is a corollary that goes like this, "Celebrate the behavior in others you want them to repeat."

The Apostle Paul used this strategy often in his letters to encourage his readers to keep doing the godly things they were doing. For instance, in 1 Thessalonians 1:6-8 he wrote, "You also became imitators of us and of the Lord, having received the word during great affliction with the joy of the Holy Spirit, so that you became an example to all the believers in Macedonia and Achaia. For the word of the Lord has sounded forth from you, not only in Macedonia and Achaia, but in every place the news of your faith toward God has gone out, so that we have no need to say anything."

Likewise, in that same letter, chapter 4, verse 1, "Finally then, brothers and sisters, we request and urge you in the Lord Jesus, that as you received instruction from us as to how you ought to walk and please God (just as you actually do walk), that you excel even more."

If someone you looked up to wrote those words to you personally, wouldn't it encourage and inspire you to want to "excel even more"?

Paul didn't come up with this principle on his own either. He first received encouragement from Barnabas, who was called "the Son of Encouragement" (Acts 4:36). And the encouragement Paul received from Barnabas clearly led to Paul imitating what he had learned from him.

This principle is so effective with our children, with our spouse, with employees, and virtually anyone. Additionally, encouraging others is simply a godly, grace-filled response to positive behavior. Encouragement should be the "currency" with which we function with each other in our families and in the body of Christ.

This topic is another one of those, "I wish I could write an entire book about just this subject!" Suffice it to say that we all need encouragers, and we should all be encouragers.

Don't Abandon Others

The "up and down" life of Peter can be seen time and time again in the New Testament accounts. In Matthew 16, Jesus affirmed Peter as a "Rock" only to rebuke him in verses 21-23 for being a "stumbling block" to Him. Then Peter denied Christ three times on the night Jesus was betrayed. This is even more astounding considering that during the Last Supper, Jesus warned Peter, "Simon, Simon, behold, Satan has demanded to sift you men like wheat; but I have prayed for you, that your faith will not fail; and you, when you have turned back, strengthen your brothers" (Luke 22:31-32).

Despite his failures, Jesus continued to support Peter. At the end of His ministry on earth, Jesus asked Peter to reaffirm his love, then promptly encouraged him and the other disciples in their future ministries. We will all stumble and fall short. We will fail one another and God. Jesus did not abandon His disciples, He remained supportive and faithful. He never gave up on people, even at the cross.

Neither will our Lord ever give up on you or on me. He sent the Holy Spirit to minister to us and to be the ultimate supporter, comforter, and encourager. He regularly intercedes with the Father on our behalf.

Who are the people you are thinking about giving up on? If our Lord does not give up on us, then neither should we give up on each other. Remember, a committed encourager will exhaust all resources while continuing to try to motivate others.

Jesus reached out to Peter as he was sinking while attempting to walk on the water to Him. Jesus didn't let him go under. Encouragers need to regularly reach out to others and help pull them up.

One of the best ways to stand in the gap for others is to pray for them. Prayer is powerful and will help unleash the power of God in their lives. "A friend will strengthen you with his prayers, bless you with his love, and encourage you with his hope."

Discussion Questions:

How could you stand in the gap for someone you know who is going through difficulties?

What are some Scripture passages that have encouraged you in the past? Who do you know right now that you could share these with for their encouragement?

Who are the men in your life who have your back and you have theirs? If you aren't currently part of such a group, waste no time in seeking to join one. Ask your pastor for leads, or simply ask another man whom you look up to, to join you for prayer and to encourage each other.

Think of three ways you could encourage someone in your family, at church, or at work?

EPILOGUE

A Clarion Call to Stand in the Gap!

During the days of the Judges, "the Israelites did evil in the eyes of the Lord," and "everyone did what was right in his own eyes." Tragically, how true those words apply to us in America today! Because of their sin, God had allowed the kingdoms of Midian, Amalek, and other eastern peoples to invade Israel and strip them of all food sources. These were numerous, mighty kingdoms against which Israel had no power. And "… Israel was brought very low because of Midian, and the sons of Israel cried out to the Lord" (Judges 6:6).

But the help God sent, came from a nobody, a guy named Gideon. When the angel of the Lord came to him, he was secretly threshing wheat in a winepress to keep it out of sight from the Midianites. The angel stunned Gideon by addressing him, "The Lord is with you, mighty warrior." God was calling Gideon to fight the Midianites.

Gideon didn't see himself as a mighty warrior, and initially he didn't have the faith to trust the Lord with what

He was calling Him to. But to his credit, Gideon obeyed, and as he obeyed his faith grew.

Meanwhile, the vast forces of Midian, Amalek, and other eastern peoples joined forces and camped in the Valley of Jezreel. Gideon assumed he'd need a large army to defeat these hoards, so he sent messengers throughout the land and assembled an army of 32,000 men.

But the Lord told Gideon, "You have too many men. I cannot deliver Midian into their hands, or Israel would boast against me, 'My own strength has saved me.' Now announce to the army, 'Anyone who trembles with fear may turn back and leave.'" And at that, 22,000 men left, leaving Gideon only 10,000!

"But the Lord said to Gideon, 'There are still too many men.'" So, the Lord gave Gideon another means by which he would pare down his army. And when he had done this, only 300 men remained!

Then, using a bizarre strategy involving trumpets and jars with torches inside, God caused the camp of the Midianites to panic, and they all started slaying each other. In this way, the Lord brought about a great victory for Israel.

My point in sharing this account with you is that it only took one man to stand in the gap for Israel, and he was a nobody at that.

 My prayer is that having read this book, the Lord has put a fire in your belly to follow Him, obey Him, trust

Him, and to stand in the gap for your family, your church, and your community. If God can do what He did through Gideon, just think what He could do with many men like you who humbly submit to Him and seek His glory!

Will you commit to being such a man? A watchman for future generations to pass along the traditional values and conservative theology that sent Christ to Calvary's Cross.

ABOUT THE AUTHOR

Dr. Jim Grassi is the founder and president of the culturally strategic Men's Ministry Catalyst, an organization he incorporated in 1981. Grassi is also the author of several books, magazine articles, booklets, and tracts.

Dr. Grassi has appeared on many radio and television programs including *Hour of Power, The 700 Club, The Carol Lawrence Show,* Cornerstone Television, Southern Baptist Television—*Cope,* Chicago Television 38, *The Dick Staub Show, Getting Together, In-Fisherman, Fishing Tales, Jimmy Houston Outdoors, Home Life,* FOX Sports, and CSN.

Grassi was born and reared in the San Francisco Bay area. Known for his evangelistic heart, he teaches people from a background of an outdoorsman, public administrator, Hall of Fame fisherman, college professor, businessman, community leader, and pastor. He has served in the capacity of a chaplain with the San Francisco 49ers, the Oakland Raiders, during Hurricane Katrina, and with the Post Falls Idaho Police Department and Kootenai County Fire and Rescue. His life experiences, study of discipleship, and work with hundreds of churches have given him a unique perspective on helping men to know God and make Him known.

His passion is to serve our Lord and assist others to know Him in a great way. Grassi is available as a keynote speaker, church ministry consultant, men's ministry leader, and life coach to those seeking assistance in developing a vision and life plan. Through his ministry website, www.mens-ministrycatalyst.org, he can be contacted for speaking engagements and assistance in developing your life plan.

OTHER BOOKS BY
Dr. Jim Grassi

Guts, Grace, and Glory

The Ultimate Men's Ministry Encyclopedia

A Study Guide of Israel

Crunch Time

Crunch Time in the Red Zone

Wading Through the Chaos

The Ultimate Hunt

In Pursuit of the Prize

Heaven on Earth

The Ultimate Fishing Challenge

The Spiritual Mentor

Building a Ministry of Spiritual Mentoring

More Than a Fisherman

Act Like Men – Be Strong

Overcoming Barriers Men Face

Beside Still Waters

The Great Shepherd / El Gran Pastor

Men's Ministry Catalyst Website:
www.mensministrycatalyst.org

MEN'S MINISTRY
CATALYST

www.mensministrycatalyst.org

OUR MISSION: To provide pastors and leaders of men with guidance, resources, and services to successfully impact men for Christ and to develop an engaging ministry to men, within their local church. Since 1981 we have partnered with pastors, churches, men's organizations and denominations to develop and implement biblically based, vibrant and engaging ministry to men. Why do we do this? Because every man deserves a chance to become an authentic, biblically based man of God.

OUR STRATEGY:

- **Develop** life changing material and models to help churches equip, connect, and engage men in issues of faith

- **Guide** pastors and leaders of men into building an engaging ministry to their men.

- **Collaborate** with groups of local churches and denominations to have a broader impact on the men of their community.

MMC offers a robust suite of innovative services and resources on relevant topics such as:

- **Lifestyle Evangelism** – Living a transparent and relational life
- **Mentoring** – Defining what it means to lead by example
- **Discipleship** – Empowering men and preparing them to lead
- **Transitions** – How to inspire and motivate men to Christ-like living
- **Intergenerational Issues** – How to develop authentic disciples that influence younger generations

---

GET IN TOUCH WITH US:

- http://www.mensministrycatalyst.org/resources
- http://www.facebook.com/MensMinistryCatalyst
- http://twitter.com/MensMinCatalyst
- http://www.youtube.com/user/MensMinCatalyst

RESOURCES:

The following are available from **Men's Ministry Catalyst**

Visit www.mensministrycatalyst.org

Contact us to learn more!

- **Weekly Devotionals for Men**: Ideal for pastors and men's leaders to email to their men. *http://www.mensministrycatalyst.org/stay-informed/devotional-archives/*

- **Weekly Tip of the Week** providing one tip – 1 minute read – that will add insight on men's issues and leading men primarily within the context of the local church.

- **Podcast** – launched on the 1st and 3rd Thursdays of the month, this 15 minute listen will add further insight to leading men, thru the expertise of MMC and many nationally known leaders of men.

- **Men's Ministry Assessment Survey:** We have the capacity to customize, process, and evaluate your survey.

- **MMC Library of Best Practices:** Especially designed to assist leaders, available at **(303) 882-5162**

- **MMC Hot-line (303) 882-5162** Call anytime for assistance on creating ministry to men.

- **Dr. James Grassi as a speaker, coach, and equipper** for individuals, men's leaders, and church congregations *www.mensministrycatalyst.org*

- **Rev. Wendell Morton as a speaker, coach, and equipper** for individuals, men's leaders, and church congregations *www.mensministrycatalyst.org*

- **Personal Church Consulting:** We will send a church consultant to your location; call **(303) 882-5162**

- **Conferences and Retreats:** Our extensive experience in providing speakers, logistics, and support for your men's retreats, conferences, and special events. Call **(303) 882-5162**

- **Speakers Bureau:** A list of qualified national speakers and sports personalities to enhance your programs. Call **(303) 882-5162**

Made in the USA
Middletown, DE
19 February 2024

49415986R00089